Alabama Poets

A Contemporary Anthology

Alabama Poets

A Contemporary Anthology

Edited By

Ralph Hammond

For Kathy Kemp —
all good returns —
Ralph Hammond

Livingston University Press

Livingston, Alabama

Alabama Poets: A Contemporary Anthology

Copyright © 1990 by Ralph Hammond

First Edition, 1990
Second Printing

All rights reserved.

Library of Congress Catalog Card Number: 90-60311

ISBN: 0-942979-07-9

Published by Livingston University Press, Station 22,
Livingston University, Livingston, Alabama 35470.

Manufactured in the United States of America.

This project has been made possible (in part) by a grant from the Alabama
State Council on the Arts and the National Endowment for the Arts, a federal
agency.

Published in conjunction with

The Alabama Reunion
———— 1 9 8 9 ————

Editor's Preface

The Greeks tell us that an anthology is a "gathering of flowers."

This collection, then, is a gathering of poetical flowers from the Alabama scene.

Its ultimate purpose is to celebrate the State's contemporary poets and to link them with a reading audience.

These criteria were used to determine the selection of poets for this anthology. They must be native Alabamians, or they must have lived at least a decade in Alabama and developed a major body of creative work while domiciled here. And, of course, their poetry must have attained a single dimension of quality.

These by no means exhaust the number of worthy Alabama poets. There are others highly deserving, and our colleges and universities are training still others yet to be heard from.

I extend special thanks to all the poets who so willingly shared their work with me during the long harvest of "gathering these flowers."

Contents

*Dedicated to the poets
whose work appears in this anthology*

John Allison

Born in Stevenson, Alabama, John Allison teaches in the English Department at the University of Alabama. His poems have appeared in a variety of magazines, including *Poetry*, *Esquire*, *The Black Warrior Review*, and *Folio*, and in two anthologies, *A Green Place: Modern Poems* and *Nothing Rich, But Some Things Rare*.

Night Animal

The female becomes the abstract.
The essential evidence is here: paths twisting
through pine, second-growth brush, swamp.
Remembering her scent sends your life into maze.

The moon, brilliant and waning,
hovers on the eastern skyline, rising
so slightly you can only imagine.
Soon you will find your legs.

The bitter food you require lies on a bed
of dead leaves. Acorns are easy to find.
For months, with water, they can keep you alive.
For now, food is secondary.

On many trails your track punctuates rich, acidic scent,
your own trap to stall her long enough
to climb her flanks, the earth and stars.
Every male night animal of your kind lures.

The one you stalled last year, you remember
her long legs flailing the night air
in a moon dance accompanied by owls.
This year she beds closer to the city than you would ever dare.

On a high ridge, on a clear winter night
the green is gone and you see the city.
Its strong lights you have seen at night
can freeze you on the highway and kill.

Now the moon is high, a lopsided world apart.
Though your eyes will fail one night, or day,
tonight they are clear, long-range cameras.
From here Mars appears deserted.

Brown hair shining in the moon, she waits,
miles away, at the edge of the suburbs.
The one who takes her, there, as you watch,
perhaps will be dead by mid-morning. Too close. Too close.

This morning your legs curl under you and you sleep.
When you wake, her lure will be stronger,
her presence more distant. No longer will she cross
clearings ahead of you sniffing for danger.

Dusk. You stir, stretch, remember.
And those who will kill you one day, for your head,
will speak boldly of your heart,
as you hang staring from their wall.

Gardening

Independence Day. My father's bean vines
slither farther up their canes every night
to hang black and full knuckled
as the fingers of a thousand field hands.

Deafening electric work and Lucky Strikes killed him,
once, but a rough doctor shook him back.
Now his tomatoes bunch like blue-ribboned hearts.
It's late afternoon and my father
will be in his garden soon.

Two hundred miles away his one son explodes
like fruit dropped dead ripe from the green walls
of a university, and plies his lover who comes
as late as dawn with delicate night birds,
toward the earth.

It's late afternoon and my father
will be in his garden soon.
Hard ground pulls at the roots
of everything he has planted.

Breathing

To touch all points in the past
is to stretch your life like a skin
to the breaking. In Tuscaloosa
with friends, the old stories are replayed
like traffic or stock car races:
crash and terminal circling.
We sit on the sofa, spectators.
On the freeways, headlines are being made.

In scrub pine, purple martins give way
to April; the slow migration completed.
Mosquito larvae in a near pond wiggle
to the surface for air, for wing.
The wind a sure carburetion.
Inside we breathe through our skins.

Inez Andersen

Born in Leeds, Alabama, Inez Andersen grew up in Birmingham. She is the author of two poetry collections, *And Now I Have Told You* and *Never Send to Know*. She was named the first Poet Laureate of the Poetry Society of Tennessee.

Weep That Wisdom Comes Too Late

I weep that wisdom comes too late. Long years
Ago the way was dark. And I, who was
A groping neophyte running the puzzling maze
Of young first love, found only alleys that
Were blind; and blocking walls of brick; and night.
Today I came upon the letters, faded dim,
From the boy who was my partner long ago
In the maze. When, trembling, I drew the letters out,
And put them straight, in chronologic way,
And then reread them all, the course I should
Have taken shone as sunlit road at noon.

So down the corridors of years I called:
"Come back, my Love, come back. I know the path
To lead you to the light. Come back. Come back."

Forever and ever a stillness follows suicide.
I weep for the dead, and myself, and Wisdom's tardiness.

What Time Is It, God?

Long, long has he lain in the timeless ground
With the timeless rain dropping timeless sound.
I ask, in my anguish, in my timeless sorrow,
For my stillborn son, has God a tomorrow?

"... Go Gentle Into That Good Night"

The Christmas Rose still holds its starry glow,
But you and I, dear aged friends, are spent.
Our petals droop as withered stems grown bent;
Now comes the winter's softly falling snow.
We feel the chill and see the clouds hang low.
December slowly spreads a snowy tent.
The time has come for our relinquishment,
For soon the New Year ends the old year's woe.
The grief and pain and darkling fright will all
Be gone. Our steps will go in velvet tread.
Since Time must turn from greening leaf to dry,
The petals of the Christmas Rose will fall
And sink into our softly deepening bed,
While we go gentle, with no raging cry.

Gerald Barrax

Gerald Barrax's poetry collections include *Another Kind of Rain*, Pitt Poetry Series; *An Audience of One*, University of Georgia Press; and *The Deaths of Animals and Lesser Gods*, Callaloo Poetry Series, University Press of Virginia. Barrax, who was born in Attalla, Alabama, now teaches in the English Department at North Carolina State University.

Poems Like This.

When things start getting away
Those first bites of time
Come out of sensations
That once set the hooks in the brain—
The lines slackening,
Inevitably losing the taste of the bait:
See how deep down and far out
The mind has to go from the bank
To bring back real bubbles for the tongue,
The most stunning pain,
The authentic feel of penetration.
Forgive me:
Even under the lull of those yellow sheets,
Yellow light,
I knew the sharks would come
To feed in the pool that flooded your room.
And even then I was thinking of the right words
For the small tactile things
That would nibble at my mind's version
Of the way things merely felt
From one feeling to the next.
Forgive me:
While you were away from me I was inside you
Trying to remember how deep,
How warm and slick, how cool.
It hasn't kept the sharks away.

All My Live Ones

Penny accepted the Alabama neighbor's green meat,
Died in our swept-dirt back yard
Near the black wash pot, her brown spot penny-
Side up. My mother's dog, but like
All pets, with no sense of justice:
After forty years she still haunts
Me, innocent of her death, with
These images. My mother en-
Trusted to me the folly of love,
The daily care of caring for them,
And the rest were all mine to lose,
Mockery in their dying
And more than fear in running away.
Rex, ears clipped, tail bobbed, escaped
Into Pennsylvania nowhere
In a cloud of flea powder for no reason
That a twelve-year-old could know.
Micky Midnight, the stray gift to me,
Sick in bed from school, black
As only cats can be, stuck it out
Only long enough for the perfect name
And took it with him.
Fulton (after Sheen the bishop
For his round skull cap), my one canary
Died so soon after he'd learned to sing,
Finally, that I wondered if song
Were worth the cost. And last: Sinbad.
One morning before Pharmaceutical Latin
In nineteen fifty-two I watched him die
My nearest death between my absent brother's
Bed and mine, stretched out, rasping, so closely
Watched I knew and remember which half-second
Distemper tore the last breath out.
But the people: how different.
Since nineteen thirty-three
I've been the key to immortality:
All it takes is loving me:
Both parents, who had me
When they were young; the brother
Who left me there that morning
Alone when that dog died;
A wife who let me go
With her life, our three sons;

7

Another wife bringing
Her hostages to fortune,
Two daughters; all the lovers.
What will I do?
They are all here. At my age what will I do
With only a bird and a dog long ago?
I cried for days. For days and days.

Eagle. Tiger. Whale.

I'm old enough to stand,
a boy in a dress looking at himself
in the long mirror of a chifforobe,
a Black child with sandy hair
tightly curled, hazel eyes and skin.
I haven't learned the words yet so I see
all the details, photograph them into my cells:
my little yellow dress with puffed pleated shoulders
and my little pearl buttons;
my little high topped white shoes and yellow socks;
my little blue ribbon somewhere.
The room behind me is dark,
nothing in the mirror but me
as in a spotlight, yet I feel
my 17 year old mother, beautiful, bending
behind me.
           No one understands how I could have seen
this: white sheets, a slim black woman is lying on her back,
a red geyser pumping from her open mouth, she stares into the
yellow eye of the ceiling. I see her from the foot of the brass
bed, from her right, my head three feet high. Someone is
screaming "Lord God Lord God he done shot the woman" while the
soft splash, splash. I stand so calm, so watchful until someone
yells "Git that chile outta here." Who knows who knows how I got
there from next door, visiting Aunt Annie over in Gadsden. It has
been a dream that neither mother nor father can corroborate, to
say it was "a shooting" that I should forget. *dont tell dont
tell* james albert's sister
whispered in the dim coal shed. she had hair everywhere.
that was the only subject, verb, object, adverb
i could've put together to tell. except
it was my birthday and i went to her yard
to pick some figs from their tree. james albert's

8

daddy said I could. i pulled a fig
And she whispered "Don't tell, don't tell"
and I felt my hand disappear into the hot full noon mouth
of Alabama's summer solstice,
its lips sucking, tongue curling around to probe
the fruit from my rigid fist.
She changed my hands from left to right,
left me partially ambidextrous and stuttering
to describe it. Now I've had wide reading,
I've made boxes to put these things in
as "reflection," "homicide," "initiation"
just as we all do *eagle tiger whale god*
and I take them out and count them, feel
their edges whenever I please and shut
them back up. But I can do this:
In the Zaire rain forest a snow leopard like a ghost leaps
and with its perfect knives
slices open this box I've made.

John Beecher

Born in New York City in 1904, John Beecher, the great-great-nephew of Harriet Beecher Stowe, grew up and for several years worked in Birmingham, Alabama. Known as a social protest poet, he has authored seven collections of poetry, including *Here I Stand*, *To Live and Die in Dixie*, and *Hear the Wind Blow*. Macmillan has published a large volume of his work, *Collected Poems 1924-1974*. He died in 1980.

Homage to a Subversive
For H. D. T. 1817-1862

Soon, Henry David, wind will fill the land
saluting your centenary. Do you
suppose that alma mater's orators
at her memorial solemnities
will quote: "What branches of learning did you
find offered while at Harvard, Mr. Thoreau?"
"All of the branches and none of the roots."
And will Concord's divines in eulogies
of you dwell on the public scandal of
your unchurched life and unrepentant end?
"It's time to make your peace with God, Henry!"
"I'm not aware," the long-faced death-watch heard
you quip, "that God and I have ever quarreled."

The pietists who con your works by rote
forswear you and themselves with servile oaths
to placate golfing clerics, bawds of the press,
snoopers, war-hawks, kept Congressmen. Silent
they stand while lying leaders make our name
odious to men, shield tyrants with our might,
huckster new-packaged servitude for freedom,
and dub the peoples' butchers "democrats."
The coffle of pampered house-slaves will dare hymn
you dead. Come back! They'll turn you in. "How should
a man behave toward this government
today? I answer, that he cannot without
disgrace associate himself with it."

Jefferson Davis Inaugural
Capitol Portico: Montgomery, Alabama

A brazen star
marks where his haughty feet were set
who later fled
in womanly disguise while near and far
the vengeful victor spoke in flame
and insult till the broken land was red
not with blood and embers only but with shame

A star inlaid
marks where he postured on the marble for a day
with his people ranged below
and seeking to stay history he bayed
the sun like Joshua
The sun impenitently set
and once more rose on irreversible woe

If I Forget Thee, O Birmingham!

I

Like Florence from your mountain.
Both cast your poets out
for speaking plain.

II

You bowl your bombs down aisles
where black folk kneel
to pray for your blacker souls.

III

Dog-torn children bled
A, B, O, AB as you.
Christ's blood not more red.

IV

Burning my house to keep
them out, you sowed wind. Hear it blow!
Soon you reap.

11

Undesirables

I lift my lamp beside the golden door
    Emma Lazarus. Inscription for the Statue of Liberty

The lifted lamp is guttering, near spent
its fuel. Double-barred the golden door
which, when it opens, opens on a chain.
Where throngs poured through, police interrogate
each refugee, admitting but the few
who pass security and kiss the Book.
Carl Schurz would be excluded with his staunch
compatriots of Eighteen Forty-Eight
whose rebel blood caused liberty to grow
in their adopted land. Could Juárez get
a visa from the State Department? Would
the FBI clear Dvořák, known to be
in sympathies an anti-monarchist?
(Deport the New World Symphony!) Martí,
the Cuban foe of imperialism? Lorca,
the anti-fascist poet? These men were all
subversive as in earlier times Tom Paine,
Pulaski, Lafayette. The authorities
would surely bar such undesirables.

John Bensko

In 1980, Richard Hugo selected John Bensko's *Green Soldiers* as the winner in the Yale Series of Younger Poets competition. Yale University Press published the collection. His poems have appeared in several magazines, including *Poetry*, *The Black Warrior Review*, *The Chicago Review*, *Carolina Quarterly*, *The Georgia Review*, and *Prairie Schooner*. Bensko, who was born in Birmingham, Alabama, teaches in the English Department at Rhodes College in Memphis, Tennessee.

Our Friend, the Photograper of Our Wedding

At the reception he photographed shoes,
hands on the punchbowl, and coats
piled on the bed. Because he learned
in school what's new is necessary,
all family portraits are fisheyed.

He said: *These are not ordinary*
pictures. You get a chance like this
once in a lifetime. At the ceremony
he got us wide angle with our heads
cut off. The justice of the peace,

who turned out to be a judge
standing on a sheepskin rug
to renew his feet, said the words.
The flash went. We kissed.
Later we found a largemouth bass

gliding from its mount on the wall
over the top of our heads had attracted
the shot. In the family fishbowl
my wife in the bulging center already
looked pregnant. *What realism*, he said.

He pointed to the shrunken figures
blurred off at the edges. *Grandparents.*
If only we could have found the way
to thank him. For that series
of the honeymoon, especially,

a hundred shots of venetian blinds,
around-the-clock on a wall-sized poster.

13

The Craft of the Lame

The lame can only go so far
before they turn into the thin
gold wire the craftsman has spun
to create the rigging of his ship.

It sits in my window, an expression
of his wish to be left alone.
When I went into his shop to buy it
he said: *The ship is not for sale.*

Because I live across the street
I have watched him all winter
coming slow like a man on crutches to work
and leaving after dark.

In the shop I watched the carrousel he had made
as the blue and purple backs of the glass
horses turned from the touch of my hand.
How much for the ship? I said. He waved his finger.

The gesture must have meant: *anything . . .*
but anything will not be enough.
He has remained faceless,
almost undefined in my memory, except

as a heavy coat, a hat pulled low
over the head, a pair of illusory
crutches. Then the finger waved again, *yes, maybe.*
A voice said: *The ship is not for sale, but this . . .*

I remember the persistence with which I stayed
as he moved around the shop
leaning toward each inseparable piece
until I thought they would fall.

The True Story

In the Philippines a man looks down
Into his bowl of soup and sees
A snake. *Waiter! Waiter!* he shouts.

The orange head lifts from the bowl
And slowly turns its dark left eye
To gaze into those of the waiter.

Perhaps the man expects the waiter
To say: *I'm sorry sir. It's the cook.
He's not been himself lately.*

Or: *Quiet! Everyone will want one.*
But the waiter calls the police
Who rush in to catch the deadbeat patron.

He admits nothing. Then, with a movement
So beyond the speed of their eyes
It might be played by a magician

He reaches into the bowl, grabs the snake,
And swallows it . . . not like someone greedy,
Like someone starved and delirious

Who finds himself suddenly at the mirage
Of the rich man's table, and then
Finds himself eating in a bed of snakes.

He is better than they will ever be.
There! he says, holding out a point of space
Before their astonished eyes,

Now where's your evidence?

Richard G. Beyer

Born on Long Island, New York, Richard G. Beyer has lived in Florence, Alabama, since the early 1960's. *The Homely Muse*, his first collection, was published in 1973, and he later co-authored *Scrod I*. He is managing editor of the literary magazine *Negative Capability*.

Reunion

> *Times I take the Salmons from*
> *the shelf and pray Occasion*
> *comes tomorrow . . . or today.*
> from the poem "Occasions"
> by Marjorie Lees Linn,
> Alabama Poet, 1930-1979

The remaining possessions of your life
Are cataloged, stored here in my closet
Where you live now in a corrugated box
With your name in large black letters . . .
There are poems we never saw or heard,
Prize certificates, newspaper clippings,
Stories, articles, letters, and photos.
It takes eighteen hours to read your life
But only minutes to see how many lives
You touched and brightened, the work
With your son's classes, talks to the
College students, poet-in-the-schools,
All the odd balls and the lonelies that
You always calmed and soothed and mothered.
It is almost like being with you again,
Poor dear poet in love with a blind world.
But, after all, these are only remnants of
Your love, yellowing paper artifacts, so . . .
Times I take the box down from the shelf
And pray Reunion comes tomorrow . . . or today.

The Silent Harbor

In measured ebb and neap the flow repeats
On marshy banks, a stoic heron stands
In morning's ashen light, and mist retreats
Exposing gray and pungent naked lands.
An osprey floats on unseen shafts of air
Above these boats, upturned in tidal sweep
Upon a timeless beach, and absent there
Are those who chart an endless tranquil deep.
In limp and tattered shreds the rotting nets
Shroud sagging piers, and weathered tackle lies
Beneath a saline crust; a gull forgets
To pierce the solitude with plaintive cries.
The sandbar shifts to stitch the scene complete
And here the water weaves from salt to sweet.

Margaret Key Biggs

Born in Needmore, Alabama, Margaret Key Biggs is the author of five collections of poetry. Her most recent, *Plumage of the Sun*, was published by Negative Capability Press. A retired teacher, she owns a home in Cleburne County, Alabama.

Below Freezing

They chilled somewhere
between silver and gold
as anniversaries go;

now his disillusioned breath
frosts her ear,
and her freezing bitterness
claims any mellowness
they once had.

Like two icicles
hanging on the same eave,
yet not quite touching,
they wait for one of them
to crack and fall.

Three Words in Green

When Hitler was raping the world,
my sister-in-law, Virginia,
embroidered words upon my blouse.
I stared at them: *amo, amas, amat*,
and found them as strange as our town,
one without men except very young or very old.
What language is that? I asked.
Latin, she said. I love. You love. He loves.
It was the only Latin I would learn,
and all I have needed to know,
the one possible antidote for war.

Steven Ford Brown

A native of Florence, Alabama, Steven Ford Brown is the author or editor of several books, including *Contemporary Literature in Birmingham: An Anthology*; *Heart's Invention: On the Poetry of Vassar Miller*; and *The Sky is Guilty of an Oblique, Considered Music: Poems, Prose Poems and Translations*. He lives in Boston, where he serves as publisher of The American Poets Profiles Series.

Summer, That Massive Blue

for Virginia Pierria

Summer, that massive blue dirigible, has floated
over the city to occupy for three months this
single piece of real estate. In the clear heat
of the summer night I fall through the six white
coffins of my father's body to sleep in the grave
of nothingness. This is memory. This is memory and
bits and pieces of the past drift away as I row out
on the great, black body of darkness. I am a white
bone star, a boat of ash and light returning home
as nostalgia goes off like a dizzying flare in my
chest. The wind, old and diabetic, alone with its
failed memories, blows through the orchard loosening
the leaves of the burning trees one by one. The sun
nails itself back up into the sky. You are disconsolate.
I try to comfort you as light, furious in the morning
window, streams through our bodies. I try to explain
to you the loss of those people and things that matter.
I try to explain that together we are happiness multiplied,
that I alone can drive away your loneliness, that we
must marry our hearts, those solitary brides,
to the wonder of the world. I lean into you, a rough
invasion. You tell me over and over that you're the
victim of love's bad humor, that you can no longer
tolerate the single sterile song of grief, the sad
neck of collapse. You turn to me as out of the clear
and absolute light of morning the dead, wings lashed
to their magnificently sleek and powerful bodies,
rise into the sky. You are disconsolate. I lean into you,
a rough invasion. The light, furious in the morning
window, streams through our bodies.

19

Things Are Being Built

Things are being built. Across the lush,
green lawn, things are being built.
And the silence, perfect and clear,
dazzles in the aftermath of each
hammer blow, each encounter with the
real. The world extends only as far
as the eye can see, as far as the
imagination has mapped. And in each of
these small countries connected to the
senses bloom fields of love and wonder
that inform the heart with desire.
We shall all bow down and be grateful
for that which is given. The blue sky
blooms, the sun bearing daily witness
blooms, the whole world blooms. Things
are being built. The silence, perfect
and clear, dazzles. And we, inhabitants
of the small countries connected to
the senses, wait each day to be taken,
for a sign, for a chance to stand as witness,
for a chance to be dazzled by the real.

From Love Embrace of the World: Frida Kahlo Triptych

> *The paintings of Frida Kahlo are like*
> *a ribbon tied around a bomb.*
> —Andre Breton

1. The Accident (September 17, 1925)

We took the bus to Coyoàcan after school. Rain
came and went, but even in late afternoon the
sun was still trying to break through the clouds.
The bus stopped in the middle of Mexico City at
Cuahutemotiza and 5 de Mayo, at the corner in
front of the San Juan market. I was holding
a balero and my sketch pads and watching a woman
in the market sort fruit. A cloud of birds passed
over the church steeple. The electric trolley
hit the bus in the middle and kept moving forward.

20

I dropped my sketch pads as the bus burst into
a thousand pieces.

It was as though the sun suddenly leaned down
and clapped its hands and the world was filled
with blinding light. I remember lying on the
floor of the bus amid the wreckage and crying people.
The iron handrail had broken loose and pierced me
the way the matador's sword pierces the bull at the
end of the beautiful but wicked ballet. The impact
tore my clothes away, and I was left wearing only
a blood dress sprinkled with gold dust from the
housepainter's torn packet. When they saw me lying
there in the wreckage, a small, dark girl covered
in blood and gold dust, someone cried out, *La bailarina,
la bailarina!* God's face drew near and just as quickly
was gone. They drew the iron rail from me and later
said my screams drowned out the sirens of the ambulances.

They thought I would die and gave me last rites
at the Red Cross Hospital. The iron rail had pierced
my side and exited from my vagina. My spine was
broken in three places, the pelvis in three places,
the right leg fractured in eleven places, and the
foot dislocated and crushed. I have joked since that day
that I lost my virginity on the bus to Coyoàcan.
Sometimes I think of that day as an enormous puzzle
with all the pieces flying apart to never be put
back together again. I should have died that day.
But I wanted to live. And when the black angels
came for me I joked and taunted them. The iron fist
of it all hits me in the chest now just to think of it.

One day I was but a schoolgirl in love with
Diego Rivera. I lived in a world of color
and motion and schoolgirl things. And then,
as if a lightning bolt materialized into
the world, as if the sun suddenly leaned down
and clapped its hands, all the world's hard
outlines became clear. All mystery disappeared.
And one Frida died and another took her place
to live on and occupy a fierce and painful planet,
as transparent as ice. And from that day I carried
inside my body a desert in which nothing would grow.
At night I dreamed of the bloody children aborted

21

into the streams of darkness. Now, sometimes, in
the heat of a summer day, I feel faint and have
to stop. I lean against the rail of the fountain
in the plaza and put my hand to my forehead to
shade my eyes so that I can see. The sun is just
inside the grey clouds, and the birds are flying
over the church steeple. I see myself lying in
the wreckage. It's as if the sun had suddenly
leaned down and clapped its hands. The gold dust
falls slowly through the resonating air. And
among the crowd, louder now, I hear someone crying,
La bailarina! La bailarina! La bailarina!

Lynne Butler

Lynne Butler lives in Florence, Alabama, where she serves as Poet-in-the-Schools. Her work has appeared in a variety of magazines, including *Cottonwood*, *The Panhandler*, *Alabama Literary Review*, *Beloit Poetry Journal*, and *Cimmaron Review*.

Estate Sale

for C. E. B. 1907-1986

At the edge of town the oil rigs lie idle,
the rusting bones of better days.
In Verna's Place the men linger over coffee
and all the talk is of hard times.
This you'd have understood, depression boy
who left home hungry at the age of nine.
Or so you said. Teller of tales, we despaired
of ever getting the truth. From the back
of ice wagons to the skeletons of skyscrapers
you made yourself the hero, then lit out west
in one of the big Buicks you loved to drive.

Cleaning out the house we become detectives
sifting clues. The swashbuckler of your stories
leaves a trail: jogging shoes for a man
who could barely walk, Chivas Regal for a man
who never drank. The man who built Camp Funston
has left hammers in the bread box, levels in the rafters,
artifacts from a life always a little out of plumb.

We fling open closets, attack the tangle
of papers that not bankers, lawyers, or daughters
can untie. Every drawer is a reproach. Years
of presents, unopened ties, unworn gloves, testify
to our need to hold you and yours to run away.
You bought love while we railed long distance,
weaving our anger into the net we all balanced above.
A letter from the grave admonishes,
"What I did, I did freely, in my right mind.
No action should be brought." Good girls,
we mind you even now.

We tag the furniture, sell the couch we threatened

23

out of spite to piss on to the termite man
for forty dollars, then knock off five
for the missing leg. The anger,
like a braid come loose at the end,
unravels. We sweep the house clean, crate
that part of home we cannot bear to leave.
We begin to tell our version of the father.

A Story

We string our lives, like beads on a strand,
story by story. My mother, my grandmother,
waiting at the door, looking across the fields
toward rising storms, talked about the year
they lived on watermelon money, how they'd
hang wet sheets in the door to cool themselves,
how it never helped. They'd tell about
the night the dogs, frantic at their chains
barked until morning, and in the light
how they found circles of tracks around the house,
deep and deliberate—mountain lions
up from the river or down from the bluffs
drawn by the fresh meat they'd hung on the porch.
Riding home I always wanted to hear that story
again. And once, jerked from sleep,
saw, I swear, a lion on the road. A story
I tell with some reserve, for there are always
those with their own version, who choose
not to see the flash of eyes beyond the headlights.

Hearts and Flowers

The valentine queen of the Shady Rest Home
is crowned with foil and paper hearts.
At any moment she could raise her scepter
to let the ball begin. The other revelers,
arranged around the edge of the hall
like a sagging fence, seem to be waiting
for the first strains of music or for permission
to leave the room. But the king can't be bothered.
He slumps in his wheelchair, a piece of cake
forgotten in his lap. He is thinking about
his tractor, the way the rabbits erupted before it,

the way the dust swirled behind, how that dust
could swallow the whole field. He has plowed
all day and would like to stop for supper,
but the field seems never to end
and the fence keeps moving away.

Ann Deagon

A native of Birmingham, Alabama, Ann Deagon is the author of ten books, six of them poetry: *Carbon 14, Poetics South, Indian Summer, Women and Children First, There is No Balm in Birmingham,* and *The Polo Poems.* She has been Director of Poetry Center Southeast since 1980 and is also currently Hege Professor of Humanities/Writer in Residence at Guilford College in Greensboro, North Carolina.

Moving North

The Brown Recluse, also known as the Hermit Fiddler, a spider whose bite produces a gangrenous sore, is apparently spreading northward. From its original home in the Southwest it has now migrated as far as North Carolina.

Not it. She. The one with eggs.
Demographer with the future in her belly,
moving up in the world. Texas rots
dry, Louisiana wet. Twenty
years in Alabama: closets, drawers,
silver chests, the backs of portraits
cottoned with eggs and everywhere the sweet
festering scent. In Tennessee
she homed into the woodpile, roughed it,
budded the boards with eggs. Now here
holed up in my ornamental block
she babysits a quiet contagion.

                     Lady,
I know your bite. I am myself
something of a recluse and given
to wearing brown. My Odyssey—
no, my Penelopeid up the dry
shins of girlhood to the wetter parts
was not unlike your own. We are heading
both of us north. The cold, I hear,
is shriveling, the cold bites back.
Even in this lush midway state I feel
a touch of gangrene on my hither leg,
some deadlier hermit fiddling in my brain.

A Gynecology

I   *There Is No Balm in Birmingham*

Among the agents used by counterfeiters
to age their stock are: glycerine,
whale oil, rose water. I know this art.
To make their tender legal, to pass current,
my petaled, my limpid aunts
distilled in the coiled copper of their afternoons
animal, vegetable, mineral
into a balmy essence that preserved
their beauty moist.
                         Leathered as I am,
Aunties, sisters, I smear my page
with crafty balsam, beauteous conceit,
hide to the last, last line the truth that's not
beauty but bone. bone. bone. bone.

II   *Customs of the Esquimaux Women*

They do not stalk the caribou
tall-boned over hard white.
Kneeling fur-trousered low to
the bleak of ice they cut one
pure hole, prise up its flat moon.
In under sea the muscled seal
like dark pigs root for air.
One woman loosens furs, dips one
bare breast into the breathing hole:
its nipple spurts a thread of scent.
Seal veer and rise, their snouts
nudge, nuzzle, strike. The woman
screams, they grapple, tug the black
clenched beast on ice, hack off
its head, the woman's cry still coming hoarse,
rhythmic.

            Nights in the igloo she crouches,
softens stiff skin between her teeth.
Beside her in a shallow stone
seal blubber flickers the whole night.

27

How She Runs

Have you seen riderless horses
in the steeplechase continue,
fallers whose jockeys jerked
under hooves three jumps back
still take the fences, Big Ditch,
the Birches, Mill Run?
They do not know they cannot win.
The fall has whetted their will.
The light weight thrown clear, the crop's
flick stilled, the voice at their ear
the crowd's voice borne on the wind
of their own pursuit. Each leap
the heart's choosing. Only between
jumps they falter, miss
the bit. The last hedge cleared
they mill about, first surmise
what absence they carry on their backs.

The Off Season

An aged lady passes the bar window
the goiter under her chin like a pink mouse.
I jot her down, marvel how goiter grows
in the iodized sea-stink of Myrtle Beach,
remember Great Aunt Myrtle, come to die
in the sewing-room, who posed each day
naked before the pier glass and my
four-years' surmise, watched her skeleton
put off its corpulence, emerge svelte.
Afternoons she taught me the sharp stitches,
nights she embroidered her burial gown.
I drink to her memory, lift the stein
with my shaky right. Benign Essential
Tremor, they call it—meaning it's bred
into my bones, likely won't kill me.
Well, something will. New bubbles rise
to head my Pilsner. Outside each leafless branch
begets its shadow against the whitewashed wall.

Dwight Eddins

Born in Decatur, Alabama, Dwight Eddins is currently a professor of English at the University of Alabama. His poems have appeared in *Sewanee Review*, *Prairie Schooner*, *Long Island Review*, *Monmouth Review*, and *Folio*.

Drifters

On the derelict barn the weathervane
is rusted south forever. The river
obeys, dragging its pointless brush clumps
toward warmth they cannot feel.
In a tangle no different from the rest
a branch convulses: cottonmouth,
gapped fangs cocked
for the luck of the current,
for what washes luckless near,

As we have done, so many times,
almost. A random country store.
Talk falters, dies. It is the stranger
by the gas pumps as if from nowhere;
something in his eyes, and something
that is not. He asks about the road,
as though it mattered. The road leads
to the towns it has to, a minor artery.
Fingering his knife he dreams connection,
its severing climax, the cancelled flow.

Twenty miles ahead, two hundred,
a boy plays in the park, imagining
glory on nameless mountains; a barmaid
plots voluptuous escape—as if
their future languished in some boudoir
patient and arranged, awaiting
their discretion; as if

it was not hitching crazily toward them
with damp straw hair like tangled brush,
a missing tooth, a tattooed
snake alert on twitching sinews.

The Pilgrimage

Old dears rout bees
from the antebellum lawn
this splendid morning.
The pilgrims have landed.
An Indian in an oak, I watch
our dispossessors plant
their walking sticks like flags.
Organdy flares in the shrivelling
azaleas, now something less
than pink. Upstairs, a hearthstone
cold for eighty years at least.
But still they come.
There's no flame like an old one.
The tough desire that kept
disconsolate, and would not take
time's pacifying trinkets, usurps
another spring. Suddenly

my grandmother sits, ironic
in the dusk, leafing a calendar
I cannot see. 1906.
A drunk, armed and surly,
slips from a trainstep
and is chopped to dice. Not
to forgive him, not to forget
his beard's fine sculpted softness,
his dancing tendons, where woodchips
fell like sleet. Sulfuric love,
etching the ghostly resurrection
in the trees of courting-places,
in the face of the unborn son,
and at last in mine. These miles
and deaths away, there's still no refuge
from that fierce, indicting warmth.
Each dawn comes blurred
with the widow's sleeplessness;
wherever my roots search
downward, they only find
her life's dark humus wreckage.

Appalachian Sabbath

At the mountain's foot
they are begging for mercy,
flecks in a massive shadow.

Cumuli drift, and pause.
Off those white, unpeopled headlands
the Ship of Zion founders again.

Modal voices are offering
all they have been.
The husked years,
trussed with patience
as with baling wire,
are stacked on abandoned wharves.

Fantastic the clapboard churches—
Bethsalem, Siloam, Rehobeth.
Grafted to wilderness,
these are names of rest
by the father's pools,
strolls in the arbors of cedar.

The plow strikes stone.

At the mountain's foot
a cold wind is rising,
the crippled dogwood quivers.

Westward

Night after night the same dust
wafting bleached in moon,
blackening as moon fails,
as great clouds answer dust.
In the lost arroyo where they rot
the bones of Running Wolf
are making weather. Still jarred
by the calvary's thunder they signal
the slaughtered herds. Hulking shadows
wheel, stampeding the sky to echo;
and the rain begins, gentle at first

31

as the weeping of children who sense
conclusion. But it is not enough,
not yet, not even the floods loose
in the prairie washes. Somehow
the tents burn on, the air persists,
a sewer of smoke and screams.
It is time: the whirlwind, the reaping.
Creation heaves, spewing the dark tornado.
Ransacked, inverted, the Horn of Plenty
writhes to rendezvous where concrete
seals its riches. Tulsa. Omaha.
The cities of the plain sleep ripe
on the earth they smother. This vortex
wants accumulation back, wants
what this dust wants: hawks again,
their sheer tangents through sheer air;
wolves in urgent cry; the deer
filing to drink through the last light
of evening, the dust alive with hooves.

Oxford

Slow punts thread the loops
of the Cherwell, bearing their travellers
nowhere. This wavering fullness of time,
this fragile gold suspension.
Alison's hair drifts in the casual wind.
All they will ever need seems
somehow almost here, diffused
among swans and willows. Hard to accept,
that it cannot go with them; harder still
that this bright prelude is an end.
Outside these walls crowned with spikes
and broken bottles, a clock will start
and never stop. And they will watch
their lives tick backwards into chaos
while traffic chews the parks, and the idyll
pales. Smudged reflections, the ruined
glass on the walls, the mirrors of ruin.

It is the last afternoon,
and there is tea in the Master's Garden.
Carefully languorous, they drawl

their polished repartee,
posed in hemorrhaging light
for a picture that will never be taken.
And one by one they slip away
through the ancient gate, hunched
to the size of centuries ago.
The river reverts to shadow, to a time
before shapes. No brilliance
inhibits this slow dissolve of swans,
white blurs in a failing lattice.
No poem resists this silence
thickening now to take the last
few querulous birds, stragglers at large
in the sprawling precincts of earth,
their lot a signalling confusion,
their single refuge dark air.

William Young Elliott

A native of Leeds, Alabama, William Young Elliott spent most of his life teaching in Birmingham's public schools. He has published four volumes of poetry and is poet laureate emeritus of Alabama. His poetry has appeared in *Negative Capability*, *The New York Herald Tribune*, *The Lyric*, and *Kansas City Poetry Magazine*.

I, Joan, to Charles VII

Dedicated to feminists everywhere
in the hope that
they may save our world.

When I came down to Domremy
To deliver Orleans from the English,
They said I was a simple peasant girl;
And so I was, and so I remained;
But they didn't see the Flame that
        burned within me,
The Flame that has lighted all the
        peasants who have fired the world,
But most of all that Great Peasant
        who came down to Jerusalem from
        Galilee;
But you, Charles, you saw the Flame,
Perhaps because you lacked it in
        yourself,
But you never came to possess it,
        Charles,
So you wanted me always at your side,
Lighting up the dark moon of your
        soul with borrowed light.
It was not to be, yet even as I stood
        in that last flame praying
        "Blessed Jesus!" I thought of you
        Charles, and prayed that when my
        spirit left me, it might enter into
        your being, redeeming you,

34

For if you have the Flame, Charles,
    you have everything, but if you
    have it not, you have nothing;
So always the Flame, Charles — and
    France!

Maurice Gandy

Maurice Gandy's collection of poems, *An Unchartered Inch*, was published by Negative Capability Press. Gandy lives in Mobile, Alabama, where he has taught at S. D. Bishop State Junior College and the University of South Alabama.

Van Gogh: "Starry Night"

A sleeping village of people
Nestled around a steeple
Is not free from fire
And flames licking higher
In the guise of a tree.

Above hills of purple dunes
Rocks a claw of a moon,
Stars of shuddering light
And huge whorls of night
As heavy as the sea.

In all is precision
Of an objective vision —
Like the madman who painted
Himself thus tainted —
As though seen by the sane.

Anne George

Anne George, a native of Montgomery, Alabama, is the author of three collections of poetry, *Wild Goose Chase, Spraying Under the Bed for Wolves,* and *Dreamer, Dreaming Me.* She is the co-editor of *A Baker's Dozen,* an anthology of contemporary Alabama women poets.

Going Home

South of Montgomery along the interstate
redtailed hawks perch on bare trees
and watch the traffic pushing through
the heaviness of late fall rain.
Tonight I will lie in my mother's
spare bedroom and listen to pecans
pelting the roof with the circular
sound of giant periods.

My mother says she was whistling
when they came to tell her
my grandmother was dead. I don't know
why this bothers her or why
she takes the memory out so often
to study it like a map, carefully, intently.
If I were a soul newly freed
I would welcome a whistle, wrap
it around me like a silver cord,
weightless, cool. But not my mother.

Which is fine. For her each morning
the sky is real and the sun is real.
She thinks she is real so she
cleans her house and never wears
patent leather shoes after five.
And this is fine. Once in Miami she
made bathtub gin, danced, barricaded
her house against the hurricane of '28.
Afterwards, the arms and legs reaching
through sand. Were they too real? Did
they follow her back to Alabama demanding
burial each day in a world of order?

37

Now, past the Davenport-Letohatchie exit
I know she is waiting. And the lights
will be on and supper ready.
A middle-aged child, I will become
for a while what she thinks I am,
and tomorrow, wading through mounds
of damp leaves, bundled against the wind,
we will fill croker sacks with pecans
and then take them in and shell them
as we do every November for the winter
my mother says will come.

Picking Tomatoes on Sand Mountain

The pickup bounces
up a corrugated road
through patchwork, red,
gold, strips of lavender. We
touch our mouths carefully
to styrofoam cups of coffee,
sing "On the Road Again."
Then the sign "Pick Your Own"
and a million tomatoes
reflecting the sun.

We are early, the only ones.
We take our baskets, move
down the rows. Ripe tomatoes
drop with the slightest of twists.
Spaghetti sauce, I think, ketchup.

At the lip of the bluff we rest,
watch clouds bank in the west.
You bite a tomato, juice
runs down your chin. I
lie back against the warm rocks,
watch hawks wheeling.

Listen, for whatever, I forgive you.

Aunt Nettie at the Well

For seventy years you have
walked this path.
Clutching your mother's skirt
you stood
on ridges of frozen mud
and watched her lower the bucket
bouncing it gently until it
turned and cut the water.
Later it was your skirt
the younger children held
while dreams clouded
your mother's waking hours.

The well, you tell me,
was your mirror.
Here, under the chinaberry
you set up your quilt frame
and met a man
come for the cool
wishing water of summer
and you married him,
driving to Iowa City
in a '36 Chevy
counting one-eyed cars
making wishes that
didn't bring him back
from the Pacific.

Now you throw chinaberries
down the well
at a thin white-haired woman
and talk of the windmill
once bigger than the moon,
of winters when the cows froze,
leaning into fences,
their eyes wide, surprised,
and summers of dry lightning
that arced like memory
from the fingertips
of your outstretched hand.

I look at the horizon

narrow as a knife
and imagine mountains
wedged into the sky,
forests that shape themselves
to swallow the wind.
You prop folded arms
on the well's curb
like a shield
grown too heavy to lift.
"There's no place to hide,"
you say.

Charles Ghigna

Born in Bayside, New York, Charles Ghigna lives in Birmingham, Alabama, where he is Poet-in-Residence at The Alabama School of Fine Arts. His poems have appeared in a wide variety of magazines, including *Harper's*, *Playboy*, *Southern Poetry Review*, *The Village Voice*, and *The Saturday Evening Post*. *Returning to Earth*, a collection of his poems, was published by Livingston University Press.

The Bass Fisherman

He is the silent type, the mute scholar
reading the sky instead of his books,
wasting no words above the still waters,
searching instead for shades of detail,
for the sharp, deep shadows of silver,
for the subtle moves that only seers see.

He is the careful type, the peaceful brave
wrapping his weapon with string, down
and prayer, warming his sight with colors
of sunset, waiting for sunrise to show him
the way, watching the depth of each cloud
that floats on the lake of his eyes.

He is the simple type, the timeless boy
flipping and testing his first flying rod,
urging it on past limits of hand and arm
to the other side of vision and dreams,
using all of that first moment to cast
the perfect balance of boy and boat.

He is the cautious type, the prize bass
with the broken hook still in his mouth,
staring up at the lake's final surface of man,
following the drag of the feather's taunt,
waiting, waiting, learning at last
the only reward of patience, is patience.

41

Divers

We were different when we returned to earth.
Too alone in our fall to forget,
We lost all trust in the touch of gentle hands.
The dropped baby in us grew.

We listened too long to a thinner wind,
climbed too close to a hollow sun,
stood one by one in the cockpit's open door,
left our mothered souls in the fading steel
of a Cessna's shaking belly,
stepped into a hand-less world,
stretched the corners of our eyes until they spit,
watched an anvil earth fly up at us,
took our own umbilical cord in hand and ripped,
and fell like frightened spiders
who spin out frantic silk that clings to only air.

Our jarred bodies lay on a sudden fist of clay,
unwound themselves from web and line
and carried the dead fish in our feet
away to dreams of distant seas.

When Howard Became Jesus

No one in the huddle laughed
when Howard said he was Jesus,
that if we did not believe him
we were all sinners doomed to hell.
The next play was a hand-off to Howard.
Everyone, even our team, piled on,
grabbing for Howard, for the ball,
for the chance to cling to something solid.
When our boyhood heap had finally become still,
a pointed shadow drew our eyes way down the field
and there against the goal post leaned Howard,
the warm ball in his arms like a baby,
his eyes round and deep like the barrels of a gun.
Walking home, everyone was silent but Howard.
He said he had wanted to tell us about it before,
but was not sure that we were ready to listen,

not sure that we were ready to believe.
He said for the past year and a half
as he lay each night on his back,
his arms stretched out in a cross,
his feet so neatly together,
he was sure he had been chosen to lead us
in the path of righteousness for his name sake.
He said it was not luck that he had aced every test,
that the bookcase and birdhouse he built in shop class
won ribbons at the county fair.
He said that was just his way of being Jesus,
that we must learn to trust his perfect ways
and regard his saintly airs with adulation.
But we walked on in silence, each new step
so tight and full of fear we could not breathe,
could not break away and run on home alone.
At his house we stopped and watched him enter,
his eyes releasing us at last behind the door.
That night beside our beds we fell to prayer
and prayed that all that afternoon was just a dream,
that we would wake up in the morning and find Howard
in the huddle telling lies just like before.

Best Man

Flown in round and grinning, holding out
the stronger hand in every stranger's shake,
kissing all the women on the hand.
To me he was much more than just a father.
Perhaps it was the way he wore his tuxedo
or the way it turned his temples silverfox.
His cheeks were full and glowing,
smiling for me and my bride through it all,
through the starchy reminder of last year's
two attacks on his heart, going home to one more,
to the dreaded grip of an early retirement,
breathing Catholic hard beside me
in that Southern Baptist church,
wading through the thick smiles to the car,
to the small airport at the end of the dream.

Home, remembering it all before dawn,
enjoying in sleep the proud son image again,

almost touching my shoulder for luck.
Rising, staring past the shouting clock
set the night before by some brutal hand of habit.

Robert Gibbons

Robert Gibbons, a native of Tuscaloosa, Alabama, has published poetry in a number of literary magazines, such as *Plains Poetry Journal*, *Negative Capability*, and *The Lyric*. Also a fiction writer, his short stories have appeared in *Atlantic Monthly*, *Esquire*, *The Southern Review*, and *Collier's*, and two of his novels, *Bright Is the Morning* and *The Patchwork Time*, were published by Alfred A. Knopf. From 1958-79, he taught English at the University of New Orleans.

At Jo's Funeral

Though she is dead,
    and now we come to bury her,
    I wear no black.

I wear no black,
    instead green:
    to praise the gardens in her life,
    where spires of bulbs
    pushed early out of earth,
    done at last with the long wait.

I wear no black,
    instead gray:
    acknowledging ashes of fires
    that burned for her—
    kiln heat to season
    the clay of the vessel,
    sun warmth to mellow
    the liquor of God.

Evening and May

Westward the hillside sky, washed pale with light,
   stands like a wall where pines lie dark and flat,
   needles, limbs, trunks in classic silhouette,
prints with the velvet signature of night.
Eastward the pines are three-dimensional
   in greens and browns that use the going day
   against the earth's shadow—backdrop of this stage—
for look of living, minor spectacle.
What's left to me of life is patterned stark
   on bright illusions of a promised time,
   but hues and depth of past invite my dream
before the curtain of advancing dark.
   Westward I look once more, then eastward, west
   and east: possessing both, by both possessed.

Andrew Glaze

Since 1957, Andrew Glaze has lived in New York City, but for a decade he worked as a courthouse reporter for *The Birmingham Post-Herald*. His books of poetry include *Damned Ugly Children, The Trash Dragon of Shensi, I Am the Jefferson County Courthouse & Other Poems, A Masque of Surgery: Poems and Translations*, and *Someone Will Go On Owing: Selected & New Poems, 1966-1986*. In 1985, Ford-Brown & Co. published *Earth That Sings*, a critical look at his poetry.

Earl

He was twenty. He was sincerely crazy.
With his head like a half-baffled chocolate easter egg,
there he was painting my house in Birmingham Alabama
doing things backwards,
painting from the bottom up
so the new paint from above
ran down on the new paint below,
putting turpentine in the water colors.
He always jumped from the back-porch roof
to the ground—fourteen feet.
—I used to be a paratrooper, said Earl—
I came down in the war with Russia
shooting a submachine gun around me in circles,
nobody had a chance to get a bead on me—
I shot them first. They thought
I was the holy, iron-assed, frosted bird.
I won the war—

The top of the house was fifty feet in the air.
The ladder was forty.
Earl fastened a ladder to the gutter.
He nailed a two by four with wooden cleats
to the top of the ladder.
He nailed a paintbrush to a broom.
He climbed and sat up on the top of them all.
He looked like a man just out of a fountain spray
of white paint. He waved the paintbrush
over his head like a banner on top of the broom.
He yelled out over the roofs of Birmingham Alabama
—look at me up here—
Look at me! Anybody want to argue?

Dog Dancing

Big Fred Carey hobbled over to me last night
in a dream, giving his heart-sworn thunderous grin,
reminding me how he'd once paid twenty a week
as I pumped gas from a Pure Oil station in Mountain Brook—
and how one time an old man parked his busted pickup
next, on the grass—some strange, lank kind of a fellow,
whose beard was dirty, whose eye was witty,
whose truck was square in the back
closed off with a delicate netting of wire.

When he'd gotten a sack of day-old buns and rolls
from the bakeshop down the street,
he opened the veiled doors behind and called out a company
of trim little dogs like grasshopper children,
fox terriers and kindred mongrels on spindly legs.
He watched them shake themselves,
then cranked his old victrola.
Hearing its stately scratches, the dogs began to dance.

What a strange sight, to see those dozen dogs
gravely turning about in slow pirouettes, hopping,
spinning in schottisches, somersaulting over their heads.
The old man stood there, keenly, watching,
slowly nodding, bidding them persevere
with squashed bits of stale bakery trash.

They silently waited with anxious fortitude
and gnawed crumbs in the wings like refugees.
On a tiny lady dog he strapped a pink skirt.
She treadled beneath the ruffles.
While the needle squeaked a bag-pipe wail,
she did a slow and mystic spin
with paws upraised and eyes in a heavenly transit,
turning and hopping, mincing her toes below.
When she'd done her turn, she took the old man's tambourine
between her teeth and grandly made the ring
of those who watched, and took their nickels and dimes.

I saw the thought fester in Big Fred's eyes,
that this old man, who should be safe somewhere,
sucking his pipe, reading the weather—
he and his dogs were out on the whim of the world.

"One morning he'll wake up dead" he said, whisking his hands.
"I mean, all right for him, he won't know better,
but what about the dogs?"
What was there I could say that he would believe?
What did I know about the demands of art?

Nijinsky

Bending up the stairs,
dance case swung to my shoulder from the back,
I looked one flight above and saw Nijinsky
sitting on the steps—I swear—
his thighs wide-stretched and huge,
facing me with wild, high cheekbones, V shaped chin,
clinging over me like an angry scaramouche.

His eyes burned with a hollow light,
and stared in mine like a furious grievance brought to bay.
Contempt drew down the corners of his mouth,
made ploughed contours over the ridges of his eyes,
—you are too gross to speak of—he seemed to accuse
—old clot of fifty eight,
desecrating my youthful art—.

"Exercise!" I stammered.
How could I make the ridiculous word compose itself?
I writhed in the contumely of his eyes
with their ghostly fire,
so the truth came hurtling out
like a series of *tours de reins*.
"I pickpocket a taste of it, that's all—for love."

His face cleared as though with a blast of light.
He grinned, fading,
and I swear, left a fleeting thought
as the stairs grew stairs again
and a tiny wind blew.
—Nothing excuses anything—nothing—
but passion's the most forgivable greed in a thief.—

Timehorse

How strange to mount this horse of time
that once set out, won't turn its mask,
and veers and bangs
about each coming back, to something new.

For instance how you've circled home,
they give you such strange looks,
and the side of the house with its feathery shakes
is like seeing through water.

Grandpa, late last week
recounting how he lost his coat.
Hard as we listened,
he was only his voice,
of whistles and creaks.

So we say we trust in stars,
they're all that stays,
for cities break like waves.
Look, your friends that talked so much
have nothing to say but hands folded.

Now you yourself pull strangely on the reins.
Dusk falls on dusk like flickers of a film.
Money rolls in the streets
Quarters and dimes, too fast to gather them.

So you snatch from the loving cup,
but even though you try
to drink from its passing; both ways
the froth is dry before you touch the rim.

Theodore Haddin

Theodore Haddin teaches literature and writing at the University of Alabama in Birmingham. *The River and the Road*, a collection of his poetry, was published by Thunder City Press. Two new collections are forthcoming, *The Pine River Poems* and *The Brother Poems*. His poems have appeared in *Aura*, *The Eads Bridge Review*, *The Birmingham Poetry Review*, and elsewhere.

Dear Mother: A Letter

I have a letter of yours
I have never answered—
Opened today cleaning out,
An old envelope stained with linseed oil,
So you can see the green leaves
Of roses and bachelor-buttons and daisies
Of the inside—have I kept this envelope
For that reason?
I read today: "The permanent things
Are matters of the spirit and heart,"
And you tell: "Michigan is a place
Where we had definite seasons
And jewel-red crab apple jelly"
And most of all of being blessed
By two mice that ate sweet residues
Off wax in a cool cellar of spies
And jonathans that made autumn
Smell fresh all winter long.
I have a letter of yours
I have never answered—
It's the letter I write in my heart
That remembers a boy going down
Into that cellar, finding a mouse
Dead in a trap, a letter that never
Gets there, I write over and over,
A boy's haste to be right that snapped out
A life amid fragrance of apples and jams.

October Light

For Bobbie Gafford

All day the light has lain at bay
A day without wind—
Sunsets this time of year are all down,
Going down, all gold and orange,
Fire in the trees and long shadows,
A stillness and a moving silence
Between the sharp sticks and shadows,
The sour smell of fall
In the heart of light.

I heard a poet read her poems
In a cafe; on the surface
Of a glass table
The poet's head was reflected,
The circles of her glasses
Circled, and made points of light,
It was the only movement in the day,
Her hair a golden band
As seen in a cloud,
Her head turning in the glass,
Her voice, her words all around us,
Breaking the silence.

Appearance and Reality

On the hillside this afternoon,
The sun falling over the face just right,
I saw the skull of a child
Buried partly in brown grass
Wound in the throat and over the missing hair.
A white, opaque eye stared out,
An utter blank in browned skin
The other eye a dark hole in dirt
The woods had piled on its behalf
To partly cover, or barely conceal
The eternal mask. As sunlight passed,
I looked again and saw a doll's head
In grass, that stilled my breath even more,

52

The thing not merely thrown away,
But shining.
And as evening came on
And there was no turning back,
The white eye became a diamond
From the hillside, reflected
Still farther beyond,
In dry oak leaves
A bright glint

Dandelion

This dandelion now,
Made to blow away,
Large yellow weed
Of the hollow stem
We held up to our chins
Long ago, saying
"Let's see if you like butter,"
And how we duly lifted our chins
And looked under,
To see golden light appear
Where a flower was thrust.
Nobody was surprised
That everyone liked butter.
The fun was in putting something furry
Under a resisting chin.
Yet, something was started
Between fur and light
And rubbing this pollen
On each other's chins,
Not knowing one day
We would look again for that light.
Today pollen has fastened
On someone else.
Twirling this dandelion,
I finger her throat,
I look for pollen under her chin.
She laughs, like someone
Who has forgotten,
And doesn't want me to stop.

Clearing for Road

For Leslie and Peter

The wood-chips I make
As I cut down small pines and ash
Are chips and shapes of a man's desire
Like old arrowheads we find in the woods,
Where Indians aspired to some good.
These chips I hold in my hand
Up close are arrowheads that won't last.
But a man can remember
Long from those years
Sweet smell of the resinous wood,
Bitter ash.

Ralph Hammond

A native of Valley Head, Alabama, Ralph Hammond now lives in Arab, Alabama, and is retired. For eight years, he served in Alabama government, first as press secretary to Governor James E. Folsom and later as the governor's executive secretary. He is the author of more than a dozen books, including *Ante-Bellum Mansions of Alabama*, and seven collections of poetry, the latest being *Edging Through the Grass*. His poetry has appeared in many journals, including *Aura, Gryphon, Voices International, Negative Capability, Amelia, Mid-South Poetry Journal, The Greenfield Review*, and *Encore*.

Hearts Broken by Language

"Unless we read poetry, we'll never have our
hearts broken by language . . . ." — Anatole Broyard

Words come easily as bird chatter.
Rolling off the tongue, they gush
with the gusto of a leaping waterfall.
Plenteous is their number, and meaningless
all too often. Like drops of rain
spattering on polished stone, they spread
directionless, only to evaporate
in the thin air of nothing. Even the scar
of their sound is forgotten to memory.
And there is no grief to their going,
and no solicitous recall for hearing
their echo ever again. Average is their
name and stump water is their drink.

But loft me a word from off the poet's
tongue, a word to succor the turn
of grief, and tell of edging close to
graveside where sorrow maximizes its
intensity, and I will claim that word
for a heart broken with anguish, and wrest
from it a consolation of comfort—the poet's
word falling like petal-bells from off a hyacinth
bloom, sweet to savor, long with fragrance.

Along the Curling Creek

"Close by a big river,
I am alive in my own country."
—James Wright

In these stalk-wilted days I
return to the curl in the creek where,
as a youth in naked sunlit body, I
dove from overhanging persimmon
limbs, splashing a rainfall of water
over barrier banks. And today, like
a scratchy needle on a worn victrola
record, I would reverse time and relive
those soft golden moments.

But a strangeness bee-swarms over this
current-flow of today, one that breathes
of false identity. Like a phoenix
image, it resurrects times long lost to
times ago, when, stripped of burdening
clothes, I learned to swim these waters,
holding hands to the silver-glistening
rounds of an empty sorghum bucket, the
lid sealing inside a cavity of dark air—
my feet fluttering stirred water, I
swam, buoyed safely aloft in the cool
comfort of the stream.

And the curling creek, oxbowing through
the bottomland, became my friend, the
two of us burying shared secrets, save
to the listening clouds and hovering sun.
It was the happy swim of youth, arms
flailing robustly through the gift of
fresh water collected from late rainfall.

But this is another lifetime, eons
apart and separated by a flurry of falling
stars that glowed away before reaching
earthrest, and I know it is all but an
apparition whose shadow is now dead to
shadows. And the fantasy that would
beckon a return to lost Then is but an
elusive whiff of passing air, briefly

recognized as pine scent and peach blossom
that soon fades into nebulae of another
realm, older than Pleiades skirting a
moonless night. But I glory in that
sudden soft scent, holding it precious,
real to yearning, wondering aloud, where
will it all end?

The Death of Rain

Summer's greening sugar-maple leaves
curl inward, crisp to touch; the once-flowering
dogwood limbs are dead to rot;
bluebirds, silent to song, latch claws
to taut wire: dryness drains the land.
A single wind-planted black-eyed Susan
bends, waterless, its yellow petals
turning crusty brown.

I walk silently across this barren-brown
earth, hear the brittle talk of
brown-bladed grass, listen to the
rattle of dead-grass-music rising
from the parched earth.

All is dead: the death of
rain is the only constancy
breeding thought. I labor its
punishment, suck the baked air
into aching lungs, and feel the
loss of life, the strident omen
of demise.

The dark of death encumbers
the spread of leaf, limb, and least of vine,
and spells out its clanky rattle
to every listening ear. The voice
of the dove is dead upon the land
and I weep the only moisture—
tears falling upon the burned
coverlet of earth.

Rain is dead,
and the earth cannot weep.

Weeping in the Wind

A plume of light glows
in the warmth of itself—
light that isn't light, that's more
than light, exalting the great spread
of the maple tree, fiery in its
late October finery.

I reach up to touch the fire,
to feel the brightening flame, but the leaf
is cold and crisp in hurried windblow.
Yet, an evasive swarm of warmth penetrates
the leaf-laden tinge of gold and yellow,
red and pink.

I remember a tree like this,
back in the bottom land of Alabama's
Big Wills Valley. Papa had a mule,
Jesse, that balked at pulling the plow,
and papa looped a grass rope around
Jesse's nose and tied him tight to the maple tree

While he lashed him brutally with a long leather
strop, teaching him the art of obedience.
I looked on from nearside, my little-boy eyes
bulging on stem for the poor mule's
burdensome plight. And, too, I remember
a cluster of golden leaves falling,

Sorrowful-like, it seemed to me,
every time papa laid the whacking
strop to Jesse's sweaty, trembling
hide—leaf after leaf twirling down
in a variegated cascade of rare and
weeping beauty.

I would like to rejoice, this long time later,
in this plume of light that isn't light—to sit
and ponder under the torch of the fiery mass and
celebrate its color magnified by the blush
of sunlight, but I remember Jesse, and the
rising welts on his hide, under another maple
tree, weeping its color in the wind.

Sara Henderson Hay

Born in Pittsburgh, Pennsylvania, Sara Henderson Hay was raised in Anniston, Alabama. After returning to Pittsburgh, she married noted Russian-American composer Nilolai Lopatnikoff. A recipient of the Edna St. Vincent Millay Memorial Award and The Pegasus Award, she has published poetry in *The Christian Science Monitor*, *The New Yorker*, *The Saturday Review*, and many others. Her poetry collections include *Field of Honor*; *This, My Letter*; *The Delicate Balance*; *A Footing on This Earth*; *The Stone and the Shell*; and *Story Hour*. She died in 1987.

Reminiscence

Jesus said unto him, "Sell all thou hast, and
* distribute it to the poor, and come, follow me."*
And when he heard this he was very sorrowful,
* for he was very rich.*
                                        — Luke 18: 22,23

Yes, I remember, long ago,
A wandering teacher came our way.
Some said he was a man of God
And word of him was spread abroad,
So I went down from Galilee
Mostly from curiosity
To hear what he might say.

He had a strange persuasive charm
Which went completely to my head;
For I inclined to youth's extremes,
Fine altruistic hopes and dreams,
I even reached the point where I
Wanted to join his company
And follow where he led.

Thank God I thought it over twice!
A most impracticable whim—
For I have had a goodly life,
I have six sons, a virtuous wife,
Yea, I am rich in flocks and land,
And these are jewels on my hands.
I wonder what became of him . . . .

Fairy Godmother

I wonder why they're never satisfied.
One wish should be enough. I give them three.
What's the result? Almost invariably
They squander the first on greed and reckless pride,
The second goes to bolster up the first,
Or add some crowning folly to the sum;
Then with the third the whole thing is reversed
To bring them back to where they started from.

What fools (I quote) these mortals be! It's strange,
They never ask for wisdom, or for truth,
They ask for gold, or power, or revenge,
Unfading beauty, or eternal youth.
I sometimes think I'll cease all dispensations
And leave them to work out their own salvations.

The Formula

It isn't easy, being the ugly one,
Or an orphan with the cruelest of stepmothers,
Or a foundling, or the dull-witted youngest son
Competing with eleven brilliant brothers.
But if you've a magic stone, or a wishing ring
Some old crone gave you for helping her cross the road,
And if you follow the rules in everything,
And if you're kind, and don't mind kissing a toad,

You'll scale the slope that nobody else could climb
And kill whatever giant disputes your way,
And reach the impossible goal in record time,
And win the bride or the groom, as the case may be.
For this is the formula which never fails.
(At least, that's how it works in fairy tales.)

Blair Hobbs

Blair Hobbs lives in Auburn, Alabama, where she writes for *National Forum*. A recipient of an Academy of American Poets Award in 1984, Hobbs has had poetry appear in *Caesura, Due South, International Poetry Review*, and *The Circle*.

Wind-borne

The air is cool in spring. The breeze blows wind
bells on the front porch as she slowly rocks
in her oak windsor chair. Dolls' cotton white
bodies lie in baskets at her feet. A hand-
glass opens the silver needle's eye. Match-
ing the thread to the hole is hard in soft light.

On the red clay, piles of dolls lie in white
oak baskets. Others are stacked on the hand
cart by the well. Their yarn locks blow with the wind
and their skirts wave, water over rocks.
Some of her babes are twins. She matched
their cross-stitched smiles in daylight.

For years she's sewn. Memories seen through white
rainbows seep through the haze. In her daddy's rock-
away carriage she would sew. There was no match
for her love of needle work. Not even hand-
some young beaus could make her feel light-

hearted. Daddy always told her she was rock-
ribbed. "Get yourself a man," he'd say. Her match-
maker father failed. All she cared for were hand
sewn babies wearing dresses made from light-
faded work shirts her daddy threw away. White
pillow case bodies were born while she rocked.

Chores around the house hindered her hand-
craft. Mama would yell for her to go and white-
wash the fence or feed the bitties. But the wind
would blow softly and the urge to sit and rock
and sew would come. A codling moth would light
upon her hand leaving dust, dark as a match

61

burned to blackness. A flame filled her with light.
Around the bone-gray fence patches of white
clover grow. She longs to float away, to be wind-
borne, and settle with the flowers growing on rock
bed foundations. This flight in dreams matches
her joy in seeing rag children, born by her hands.

The air is still in spring. The songs of wind
bells die. She strokes the yarn hair of a milk-white
doll as she sews its last stitch with her antique hand.

A Lesson in Fortitude

Because I need
to hold power,
I test
how sharp
the knife, how hot
the stovetop's
spiral
is pressed against
finger
tips. And when
the blood
slides,
curls snake-
like into my palm,
you turn
with the dull side
of the blade,
and will
not let me
show you what
I have done.
Waking
in the dark harbor
of the flesh, a spirit
stirs,
opens one cool
coiled eye.

Andrew Hudgins

Born in Killen, Texas, Andrew Hudgins grew up in Montgomery, Alabama.
His first book of poetry, *Saints and Strangers*, published by Houghton Mifflin
Company, was one of the three finalists for the 1986 Pulitzer Prize in Poetry.
In 1988, Houghton Mifflin published another collection, *After the Lost War: A
Narrative*, a sequence of poems based on the life of Sidney Lanier. Hudgins
teaches at the University of Cincinnati.

Saints and Strangers

You teach a Baptist etiquette, she turns
Episcopalian. I did. It's calm.
And Daddy, who shudders when I take the host,
stays home and worships with the TV set.
He's scared to leave the house. Incontinence.
When he's wet himself, he lets us know
by standing grimly at our bedroom door
and reading from his Bible. We think about
a nursing home. If I put on Ray Charles
he huffs around the house and says, *Marie,*
that nigger jungle-thumping hurts my head.
But these are little things. In many ways
the stroke has helped. He's gentle with the girls.
For hours he'll ride them horsy on his knees.
Still, there are those damn demons. Mine are blue,
Jim's red. He whispers demons to the girls
and gets them so they don't know what to think
of us. Beth's asthma starts. I tell the girls,
You play pretend, don't you? Well, you can stop.
But Paw-paw can't. He always plays pretend.
They seem to understand. In some ways, though,
I think he's even purer now—a saint
of all his biases, almost beyond
the brute correction of our daily lives.
Strangeness is part of it. And rage and will.
There's something noble in that suffering
and something stupid too. I'm not a saint,
of course, but as a child I had a rage
I've lost to age, to sex, to understanding,
which takes the edge off everything. Perhaps
it's my metabolism cooling down.
Who knows? One glory of a family is

63

you'd never choose your kin and can't unchoose
your daddy's hazel eyes—no more than you
could unchoose your hand. You get to be,
in turn, someone you'd never choose to be.
When feeling strong, I'll ask him to give thanks.
If he goes on too long, I say amen
and pass whatever bowl is near at hand.
Jim carves the meat, the girls reach for their tea,
and Daddy takes the bowl and helps his plate.

Julia Tutwiler State Prison for Women

On the prison's tramped-hard Alabama clay
two green-clad women walk, hold hands,
and swing their arms as though they'll laugh,
meander at their common whim, and not
be forced to make a quarter-turn each time
they reach a corner of the fence. Though they
can't really be as gentle as they seem
perhaps they're better lovers for their crimes,
the times they didn't think before acting—
or thought, and said to hell with the consequences.
Most are here for crimes of passion.
They've killed for jealousy, anger, love,
and now they sleep a lot. Who else
is dangerous for love—for love
or hate or anything? Who else would risk
a ten-year walk inside the fenced-in edge
of a field stripped clean of soybeans or wheat?
Skimming in from the west and pounding hard
across the scoured land, a summer rain
raises puffs of dust with its first huge drops.
It envelops the lingering women. They hesitate,
then race, hand in hand, for shelter, laughing.

Loose Change

We'd sip our water and wait till supper came,
then he'd return thanks. It was never quick
or done by rote. It was heartfelt—and loud—
while everybody in the truck stop watched.
They tried to do it secretly, the way
you look at cripples, retards, droolers, freaks.

I'd raise my head and watch them watching us,
and once, seeing my head unbowed, he said,
Elizabeth Marie, please close your eyes.
He says that we are strangers here on earth
and it is true I've never felt at home.
In Denver, once, a man asked me the way
to Mile High Stadium, and though I'd been
in town almost two years and had a job
I said, *I'm a stranger here myself,*
amazed at what was coming from my lips.
Are you okay? he asked. How could I say
that I'd been talking bad theology?
But it was worse for Daddy, I suspect.
At least I watched the world and tried to make
accommodation. Since he wouldn't tip
I lifted loose change from the offering plate
to slip onto the table as we left.
Staring right at the waitress, I would think,
Take this, you slut, I've stolen it for you.

Consider

You have considered the lilies of the field,
how they do nothing for their splendor
and how they shine like moons upon their stalks,
arrayed in the exacting glory of the sun.
Consider now the mosses of the cypress swamp,
the great droop-headed grasses of the salt marsh,
and how, beneath the shadowed pastels
of the wetland flowers, there lingers a hint of violet
that fades in full light, whitens and dies
like a sin you are especially partial to
because it makes your life more intricate
and somehow better. Consider, too, the various lights
that outlast the last, hard leg of the pilgrimage
through leaf and branch, moss, mist, haze, and gnats,
are rare and changed, softened with impurities,
and should be blessed each with a proper name.
In the sun-bright fields it's just called light
because it's known there only in its scouring brightness.
Consider the dream I dreamt last night of Christ
glowing in holiness, as metal in a forge
will pulsate red, yellow, and finally white

before it starts to lose its this-world shape.
He asked me to bathe his burning face
and soften the radiance that was killing him,
and I led him to the marsh and immersed him,
almost vanishing in the steam that rose around us.
Consider: from the reeds close at hand the marsh hen lunges,
a blast of stubby wings and dangling legs,
so awkward she soon relinquishes the sky,
flashing the patch of white beneath her tail
as she bolts between the tassels of marsh grass.
And down the random corridor of water oaks
beckons the hollow, two-note fluting of an owl.

Magnolias

Alabama: the first, a girl child.
The rocking chair is cold, the porch colder,
but I could sit here for a year,
thinking of my child, her dwindling.

The magnolias too are windswept
graveward. Neither live oak nor reed
resists the weather's breath,
but each lets go its green, its living part.

Spring, when it comes, is at first wet,
becoming lush, giving way
to the darkgreen darkness
where magnolia leaves hover like wings,
inches off the receding earth.

Then the blooms on the tree will open.
They are so clearly flesh of
our flesh. Without the prolonging bone,
so clearly transitory.

When touched—and I touch them—
the blossoms smudge,
the flesh dying beneath my acid hands,
turning brown in the shape of fingertips.

Rodney Jones

Born on a farm near Falkville, Alabama, Rodney Jones has received a Lavan Award for Younger Poets from The Academy of American Poets and The General Electric Award for Younger American Writers. The University of Alabama Press published his first major collection, *The Story They Told Us of Light*, and the Atlantic Monthly Press published a later one, *The Unborn*. In 1989, Houghton Mifflin published his latest collection, *Transparent Gestures*. He is a member of the English faculty at Southern Illinois University.

Dirt

I am not a saint. All
that I am coming to
is crusting under my nails.
I am dragging my dull hoe
through the peppercorns
and letting the malathion snow
from the twin clouds
of my rubber gloves.
Here I am, the marshal
come to rescue the schoolgirls!
Here I am, the fat messiah
of the family! My aphids
twitch, of abstraction
and consequence bereft. They
linger in the narcotic hair
of the okra like glue,
their love's labor multiplied.
But I am merely exhausted
and hot. Sweat
clings to my brow
like thorns, my face
is flawed with the maps
of continents I shall never see.
My cleanliness is next to sleep.
When I look into the mirror,
when I lower my head
into the cool basin,
it is mercy I think of.
I keep trying
to grab some purity
in the water pouring over my hands.

The First Birth

I had not been there before where the vagina opens,
the petals of liver, each vein a delicate bush,
and where something clutches its way into the light
like a mummy tearing and fumbling from its shroud.
The heifer was too small, too young in the hips,
short-bodied with outriggers distending her sides,
and back in the house, in the blue *Giants of Science*
still open on my bed, Ptolemy was hurtling toward Einstein.
Marconi was inventing the wireless without me.
Da Vinci was secretly etching the forbidden anatomy
of the Dark Ages. I was trying to remember
Galen, his pen drawing, his inscrutable genius,
not the milk in the refrigerator, sour with bitterweed.
It came, cream-capped and hay-flecked, in silver pails.
At nights we licked onions to sweeten the taste.
All my life I had been around cows named after friends
and fated for slaughterhouses. I wanted to bring
Mendel and Rutherford into that pasture,
and bulb-headed Hippocrates, who would know what to do.
The green branch nearby reeked of crawfish.
The heavy horseflies orbited. A compass, telescope,
and protractor darted behind my eyes. When the sac
broke, the water soaked one thigh. The heifer lowed.
Enrico Fermi, how much time it takes, the spotted legs,
the wet black head and white blaze. The shoulders
lodged. The heifer walked with the calf wedged
in her pelvis, the head swaying behind her like a cut blossom.
Did I ever go back to science, or eat a hamburger
without that paralysis, that hour of the stuck calf
and the unconscionable bawling that must have been a prayer?
Now that I know a little it helps, except for birth
or dying, those slow pains, like the rigorous observation
of Darwin. Anyway, I had to take the thing, any way
I could, as my hands kept slipping, wherever it was,
under the chin, by tendony, china-delicate knees,
my foot against the hindquarters of the muley heifer,
to bring into this world, black and enormous,
wobbling to his feet, the dumb bull, Copernicus.

Meditation on Birney Mountain

Today I come out of the thicket tired, without words,
my thighs dragging from the long artery of the watershed,

the yellow brick-clay of Alabama gumming my bootsoles,
and, while the heart slows, think of the kit fox

slowing, gathering his haunches in the last resolution
before the kill, or how, below me in the valley,

the Fairview Church of God, the punctual hedgerows
hiding their rabbits, and the dozen or so houses

of relatives seem to float in the slanting snow
like an Alpine village trapped inside a paperweight.

After the war my father came up here with his crew
of laborers from Powell's Chapel. They hacked

and gutted. They cut a brown swath wide as a gridiron
across five blue mountains for the TVA right-of-way.

Now his labor is silent. Only the cables hum
with light that rinses the screens of televisions

with the red juice of Apples that have our numbers
coded beside our names in the Crockett National Bank.

And farther on, where humus feathers the ridgeline,
it is the woodpecker, his appetite the deepest percussion.

It is the pulse of an old word, its connotations lost,
only the worm of meaning scarring the hollow trunk.

I was seven when my grandfather first brought me here
to the big sinkhole dished out beneath the southern peak,

where he let a stone drop in 1896 and heard the *ping*
and *thit* on and on, against the bottomless pitch

of the abyss, heard, past creekwater and seepage,
the dim beast snicker from the quick of the mountain.

Now rubbish stoppers the sinkhole: bedsprings
        where we loved,
heaped beer cans turned the color of fallen leaves.

It seems smaller now, and frivolous, like the ironies
of adolescence, like the upsurging of the green testicles.

Today I climb higher to look for fossils in a boulder
that gives its age stubbornly: first, a cloudy gash

that is so much like one of those fluted scars
the propellers of pleasure boats carve into the backs

of sea manatees; and when I look closer still,
when I strip back the nibs of lichen, the nut-fleshed

ears of moss, I can make out the leaf-shape and filigreed
spines of the first letters in the language of limestone.

I can touch like braille my old fathers, the *graptolites*,
the years that harden toward me, looking at the bare

bush inside my palm, bowled over by the radiance,
the nostalgia for stars. Until I turn away

stumbling into saplings, tripping headlong into gullies,
I am thinking like a bucket falling down the well of heaven

and I come down the mountain above my mother's house
like Moses with strangely inscribed tablets.

Remembering Fire

Almost as though the eggs run and leap back into their shells
And the shells seal behind them, and the willows call back their
        driftwood,
And the oceans move predictably into deltas, into the hidden
        oubliettes in the sides of mountains,

And all the emptied bottles are filled, and, flake by flake, the
        snow rises out of the coal piles,

And the mothers cry out terribly as the children enter their
      bodies,
And the freeway to Birmingham is peeled off the scar tissue of
      fields,

The way it occurs to me, the last thing first, never as in life,
The unexpected rush, but this time I stand on the cold hill and
      watch
Fire ripen from the seedbed of ashes, from the maze of
      tortured glass,

Molten nails and hinges, the flames lift each plank into place
And the walls resume their high standing, the many walls, and
      the rafters
Float upward, the ceiling and roof, smoke ribbons into the wet
      cushions,

And my father hurries back through the front door with the
      box
Of important papers, carrying as much as he can save,
All of his deeds and policies, the clock, the few pieces of silver;

He places me in the shape of my own body in the feather
      mattress
And I go down into the soft wings, the mute and impalpable
      country
Of sleep, holding all of this back, drifting toward the unborn.

Marjorie Lees Linn

Born in Collinsville, Alabama, Marjorie Lees Linn called herself a "migrant child" because her construction-worker father was always on the move. Two collections of her poems appear in print, *Notes I Have Sent You* and *Threads From Silence,* the latter published posthumously. She died in 1979.

" . . . they live in a steady shame and insult of discomforts, insecurities and inferiorities, piecing these together into whatever semblance of comfortable living they can, and the whole of it is a stark nakedness of makeshifts and a lack of means."

—James Agee, *Let Us Now Praise Famous Men*

Outside the Shadows

Part of the whole of it,
whose feet knew floors
of Alabama clay
worn smooth and hard as slate,
whose eyes reflected light
diffused through windowpanes
of paper
greased in rendered fat
to brown translucency;
brief heir to shame and insult,
whose life held nakedness
as lightly as a dream.
Never quite believing either one.
More sure of silence
and the promises of silence.

My life holds yesterday
more lightly than a dream.

*My feet touched marble
stained with amber light!*

I stand
outside the shadows of the makeshift
and the lack.
The silence
blooms.
We sing.

Threads from Silence

In the thirties he chopped wood,
worked the land, joined road gangs,
shoveling dirt for fifty cents a day,
with any luck.
He had mouths to feed,
a wife
and, one by one,
five skinny kids.

For love of these he faced the wind.

When he was fourteen,
an ancient, jagged hedge
gouged his left eye out of place,
carving flesh and crushing bone.
The neighborhood M.D. patchworked the wound.
He kept his sight.
But the eyelid never worked the same,
it closed halfway
and froze.

Now, day after day, the wind flung dust
into the injured eye
that teared against the onslaught,
streaking grime along the nose, the cheek,
scalding ragged scar,
while he kept silence and a suffering
he thought he bore alone.

His oldest child,
the one who took to books and fantasy,
began to weave a sheath
of threads she gathered from his silence
to encase her dreams
and pocketed a prayer,
for all the years to come,
that on whatever space of land he faced the wind
it would pass
and hold its peace.

Rick Lott

Rick Lott was born "at home" in Beaverton, Alabama. His work has appeared in many literary magazines, including *Kenyon Review*, *Poetry*, *Carolina Quarterly*, *Kansas Quarterly*, *Texas Review*, *Poetry Australia*, *Western Humanities Review*, and *Southern Poetry Review*. In 1984, Anhinga Press published a collection of his poetry, *Digging for Shark Teeth*. He has received two awards from The Academy of American Poets and was awarded first place in The Hackney Literary National Poetry Awards. He is a faculty member in the English Department at Arkansas State University at Jonesboro.

Nocturne for Autumn

Sitting on the front porch when the evening
Is spilt light soaking into the ground,
I come after many years

To a book that is an abandoned house
Where darkness sings in the corners, a house
That echoes the silence of other lives.

Like winter grass, mold grows on the cover,
And faces line the pages in rows
Even as headstones. After the light

Goes, my fingertips touch a face
In the warped and musty paper
The way a blind man's touch a lover.

Astonishing as the moon
That swam into Galileo's lens,
She once commanded the tides of my body.

Now the harvest moon looms above
The elms, the pale face of a stranger
Who comes as in a dream to say:

I am your lost youth, risen
From its bed of dust to startle you
With the ageless faces of the forgotten;

I am the one you love, though you will never
Know, the black tracks in snow that lead
Nowhere, though you follow until you wake.

Distant as my own image in a mirror,
The dwindling moon stares back,
Until I shut the book and go

Into the dark clasp of the house,
Knowing we must go on reaching for others,
Though each embrace is irretrievable,

And a lover seen across the room
Is light from a body already in the past.

Lucy Audubon Speaks to the Night

Insistent as creditors, rain taps the window.
As I lean to blow the candle out, shadows
Wing against the walls of this room
Lent by the woman whose children I teach.
Many from Bayou Sarah have fled yellow fever
To these pine woods, where I wait
For my fledgling husband to fly.
An infrequent visitor, he is still
The reckless boy who tucks his fiddle
Under his arm and dances all night,
Time after time abandons his family
In some backwoods cabin while he seeks deeper
In the wilderness for unknown species.
Failure always drives him back to me,
His shaggy head a nest of hopes and plans.

His journeys' sole profit are strange tales.
Some seem my memories: once on the frozen
Mississippi, large flocks of swans gathered
And lying flat watched wolves creep up,
Until the swans trumpeted in alarm, spread
Their wings and ran, thundering on the ice,
Then rose.

He writes that color fades from dead feathers
Almost as fast as it drains from dead faces;
So in warm weather he quickly sketches

75

Fresh-killed birds, skins them, and preserves
The feathered hides in rum. He loves
The bay-breasted warbler, mockingbird, shrike,
And his beautiful drawings collect like debts,
But do not gratify his desire to own
Living beauty. In my recurring dream,
Blackbirds rise like smoke, and he wades
Through marsh toward a white heron posing
In the evening light for this final shot,
Then gathers the drooping bird in his arms.

The Gardener

My father cultivated silence
In his cactus garden, spent summer nights
Drinking at a redwood table in the center
Of his thorny geometries,
Watching the night-blooming cereus.
At Easter he travelled to the Dog River
To swim its span and fish the lily pads.

When my father stripped to swim, the roses
In his pale skin astonished the green air.
The day they bloomed, mortars covered a field
Of snow with sudden black blossoms that shook
Their pollen on the soldiers huddled there.
The snow sprouted strange flowers then.

My father always came out of the water
The same man who dove in, unable to douse
The rose of fire in his head.

Now we shovel the ash under,
And pray the lotus blooms in his mouth.

The Man Who Loved Distance

The entire country afire with spring
clearing, distant mountains loomed
as shadows in the blue haze,
and the fetid smoke followed
me everywhere, slunk
into the hotel dining room,
trailed me into my room and crept between
me and the sleeping girl from the Alemeda Bar.
All night the ceiling fan squeaked
like bats in the darkness above the bed.

In a dry season, in a scorched country,
I wandered dusty streets, afraid to try
the sweet drinks souring in big jars
on the pushcarts of doleful vendors.
Poincianas billowed flame.
Orange peels and mango hulls rotted
under the listless smoke of flies.
A boy with a bloated belly
held out one cupped hand of nothing,
and the fish in his eyes swam away.

Palm fronds drooped, dead wings,
in light that splintered on the bay.
Fishermen's dugouts lay like lost souls
on the burning sand. In the market,
fish stacked on banana leaves stared
after me, and people in the streets
slid away from my camera.

Fondling the passport slung under
my shirt, I boarded a plane and rose
into the heavens.
I cupped a tumbler of gin, averted
my gaze from the bruised land
below. The somber odor of smoke
embraced me all the way home.

Susan Luther

A native of Lincoln, Nebraska, Susan Luther has lived in Huntsville, Alabama, for the last twenty years, where she is a part-time English faculty member at the University of Alabama in Huntsville. Her poems have appeared in *Negative Capability*, *Kansas Quarterly*, *Cumberland Poetry Review*, and *Piedmont Literary Review*. She is the assistant editor of *Poem*.

Two Views of Howard's Chapel

a memorial to Sally Howard
constructed by Col. Milford W. Howard
at the North Entrance of De Soto State Park, Ft. Payne, 1930's

i

There is this huge
knuckle of God—at least
somebody thought so—em-
braced by a chapel. Somebody

built the building right around
one of the biggest rocks you've ever seen.
It's huge: much higher than a woman's
head: and outside the cross-topped jagged block looks
like some—I don't know what—some stone-
skinned hybrid out of "Star Trek"—devouring
civilization like a cinema sarsen.

Really, who'd conceive a ridiculous thing like that?
At least it attracts the tourists—
and campers, I suppose,
on Sunday morning, all sweaty
from hiking the path by the river
to get there, in muddy jogging shoes
and dusty jeans. Their jaws must hang wide

open when they see the whole back wall and altar
is the enormous behind of that overweight rock
(They must think: "It takes an Alabama redneck!")—

There's some verse or other on it
out of the Bible, or something. Really

78

you ought to see it—we'll come up
next time you visit—

those little yellow flowers by the doorstep—I've never
been sure of their name—ought to be in bloom
about April. And the churchyard—it's so quiet there—
looks so peaceful, this time if year.

ii

IMMORTALITY

God Has All Ways Been As Good To Me As I Would Let Him Be

When the rough pines burr
their wind songs
God's just clearing His throat

& if His funnel bell should sweep
the mountains clean
eventually   He will make them new

new trees, new mountains   All things
the Lord hath made
& unmade He shall remake

Take me into your heart oh God
the stony fist
schist chrysalis

and cupped hand budding
to silk-brush   & a burst
of seed   Lord

conceive me   bear me
as the child
who would be found

Lord, I pray make me happy.
But God don't let me forget how I cried

79

John McMoy III

John McMoy was raised in Montgomery, Alabama. His poems have appeared in *Midwest Poetry Review, Crossroads, Amelia, Scintillations, Soundings*, and elsewhere. He operates a real estate investment company in Marietta, Georgia.

Intermezzo

I

My objection to possession is my absence,
drifting alone at twilight, lying face-up
in a boat on a private lake.
I smoke a cigarette as slow as love,
blowing smoke into the moon,
the mouth of this bell jar.
It isn't hard to imagine it:
implying boundaries that
really do exist, forming the place
where night sounds echo
in vertical planes, moving in
walk-through rehearsal
of something or everything primordial.

II

No meanings can be sought
or created without another being
on whom to impose them,
so time turns further and further back,
pursuing itself and discrediting
the bacchanalia of light and glass,
which you can keep for yourself.

I am blanketed by occasional gales
of insect hum, the cadences of reeds,
the sudden karate blows of trout
breaking the black surface.
And you—you I can imagine
watching the boat adrift
in a mosaic of Paleolithic lines
and shadows, wondering why I would
choose the tainted symbols

80

of an unknown lake over evenings
in town, teas at three o'clock,
the matinees on Sundays.
"You are merely the victim
of infantile obsessions,"
you would probably say, "a wanderlust
you should have outgrown."
But the choice is my own,
falling centuries now in sleep,
drowning, drowning if I wish
in a madrigal of night.

Tableau: 1968

I wait in the den as if backstage while
Mother washes the dishes. She is invisible,
but I hear the faint syncopation
of plates and silver colliding in slow motion,
spheres in her own indifferent galaxy.
Halcyon days went out of style with Yeats:
She senses it. Her thought rises free
and wordless like a jaunt in an open car,
free above the drone of the evening news.

That is how I picture her:
frozen in a black-and-white photograph,
her laughing face lifted toward the sun.
She becomes twenty, blind to the lacerations
of a nation at war, retrieving threads
of half-remembered loves in quarries
of time-past. I know she is of
another place even as I wait,
her thought far away as the news
beats death like a metronome.

James Mersmann

A native of Richmond, Kansas, James Mersmann has taught American litera-
ture and creative writing at the University of Alabama at Birmingham for the
past sixteen years. His poetry has appeared in numerous publications, including
Kaleidoscope, Aura, Sunflower Petals, and *Contemporary Literature in Bir-
mingham*. Thunder City Press has published a collection of his work, *The Isis
Poems*.

Leaving Home

In Kansas City, too, the stockyards
and shambles lie at the dark center—
from the black of the bull's eye
the city swirls buildings of white bone

The slaughterpens of Wilson and Swift
and Armour Star, steam
with a thousand bawling cattle,
and on each forehead swirls

a center of grace, a miraculous
god's eye of tufted hair
a target,
and point of departure

At great gray Cudahy
in stench thick as noise
the Hereford bull
shies into the knacker's chute

wide-eyed, flaring wet nostrils
at the terrible floor
and before his head can lift
—there! that rose-star of soft hair—

the mallet slams him splay-legged
a sudden black wall widens
loud in his skull
huging his eyes, stunning stiff time

to incredible slowness
his locked legs, rigid as a rocking horse,

quiver and hold, almost forever quiver and hold,
buckle and he falls
                    & falls

and falls
slamming the final floor
a hook through the nose
skids the body forward

grapples the heels, jerking
the heavy butt rafterward
in a screel of pulleys,
.the twisted neck, the nose smearing the concrete floor

then he feels a thin, hot,
gold thread drawn down
the seam of his belly
and watches the gut gutter
filling with his own entrails

until in the dimming cave that he is
a cold red wind begins to ache
and his upturned, filming eye
draws tight with surprise
at such hunger

The Gift

In this unlooked for,
unasked for moment,
sitting at the kitchen table
looking into the next room,
I all at once see what has been there,
how long?

Sunlight fills the room corner
in a geometry of shadow and brilliance,
lifts the picture molding,
the shining hinges of a door
the white mopboard,
and in my own simple house,
empty of everything,
I am Vermeer and Van Eyck

and the spirit lives in white paint
and light and blue wall
and through the angle
of a yet farther door and farther room
and window, a still
different distant sky,

and in the middle ground
a fishbowl, collecting light
like a dragon in bliss!
reflects lintel and post
and blinds, and a red bow
from the child's hair
discarded on the white table.
Light like a blade on the wall,
in the fishless water and bowl
bounced, and arced, and repeated.

I look down to write this,
and look up, and am amazed,
in one moment the light has gone,
and except for my eyes,
and these words,
never was.

Singing of Black

All these years I have lived in bright rooms,
the night has leaned against the locked windows
like a lonely woman, and I have not seen her!
The windows squaring the dark
gave me back
my small self
in the lamp's light

Now I stand in the door
framed by light
and feel the dark's dark eyes
her long fingers softly learning
the curve of my shoulder, the slant of my thigh

Lithe daughter, Isis child,
because you have given yourself

to me, the night is full; I open
my arms and my mouth to the darkness, my lungs
heave with the night's breathing

Now the night and I love each other!
She refuses to leave me, even in the day—
she hangs on in the dark sheaths of my shoes,
in the whorl of the shell from the sea,
in the cup of my own hand!
Yes, now, naked and lovely, and singing of black,
she bathes all day in the well of my ear

William Miller

A native of Anniston, Alabama, William Miller is now completing work on a Ph.D. at the State University of New York at Binghamton. For several years, he taught in Jacksonville State University's English Department. His poetry has appeared in several publications, including *The Florida Review*, *The Laurel Review*, *The Southern Humanities Review*, and *The Dan River Anthology*. He is co-author of the chapbook *The Trees Are Mended*.

Shiloh Cemetery
(Delta, Alabama)

In all directions
the land has been sold for pulpwood.
This stand of graves
with its one live oak
is the exception to every rule
drawn by distant timber companies.
Here nothing is cheap
or easily disposed.
The monuments
have taken root,
bloom like marble flowers
in the heat of an August day.
Mica glitters
in the pattern of a promise:
untold wealth below this soil.
The headstones themselves
lean together
like old conspiring women
across a fence.
Stories told and retold
on summer air
are myths undisturbed
by the sound of distant sawmills.
No one harvests the weeds
grown rank and glorious
or the tree that aspires
to unthinkable heights.
Even the dust beneath rotted boards
has dreams at Shiloh Cemetery.
The dead's returned to claim these hills.

Old Faith

In this room
of sackcloth and whispers,
wrists cross above brown boards
a confusion of bodies.

And fear
like the snake itself
unfolds in air—
a living circle
cold to the touch.

They have this
and Sundays by the river:
the backward plunge
in steep water,
the heat that dries
their drowning from this world.

But for every hymn
sung in mountain air,
a bullet goes unfired.

The weeks are flat
as hard roads between
one pump town and the next.

Machines glitter in windows
like an old dream of harvest—
more than dirt crops,
the land converted this time.

And on the square
the courthouse stands open
as ever.
Gray at all angles,
it fades from lack of paint.

The sun keeps his sky
and the earth belongs
always to the godless.
No man prays to himself
with a serpent in his hands.

His fields are small
but enough.
When he drinks from a dipper
he tastes the iron of greed
then walks his anger into dust.

That rumbling across the ridge
is not an army moving,
dry thunder only.

He kneels among weeds,
hopes to be bitten.

Haynie's Well

He fell to forgotten water.
Twenty-one-years old, a slave
he remembered in the weightless moment
a story familiar among blackened rows.
House of stone, candles at dusk,
clothes and a safe passage.
But the well
like so many things
was forgotten in the high grass
beyond cotton.
His run through hot acres
ended in a pool of dissolving dreams.
Neck snapped
his eyes followed
the faintest circle of light.

Another's bones join his
and another's.
Silent company for the longer journey.
The fields overhead
fade in the twilight of columns.
The stone house darkens
except for fleshless grins,
candles reflected
across the surface of found water.

Carl P. Morton

A native of Leeds, Alabama, Carl P. Morton was Alabama's Poet Laureate from 1983-1987. He is the author of two collections of poetry, *Desiring Stone* and *An Occasional Tiger*. His poems have appeared in several publications, including *Scrod I*, *English Journal*, *Negative Capability*, and *Alalitcom*.

Could Such a Giant Live Here?

(an impression on visiting Shakespeare's home)

Here Will? Bound by dark walls and cubicles
within this drab-oak shroud that you called home,
hugging this rude-stoned hearth as evening dulls
hoar English countryside, as winters come
to haunt dark moors and wreathe them in grey fogs
of Hamlet's own soliloquies, was here
where genius grew to dream, to quill such logues
of witches' brew, of laughter and of tear?

Did such a giant live here to bend and stoop
thru needle doors and creep this creaking stair
to bed his Ann above? This narrowed coop
might once have closed upon him unaware
and made Macbeth a living morbid thing,
but how induce an Ariel to sing?

Our Lady of Compassion

(For Marjorie, who willed her body to Medical Science)

I could not forgive you until now,
knowing the tank where your public body lay,
your memory sweetened with formaldehyde
to leaven up inside my fermenting thoughts
     like your drowned cadaver,
      surfacing every five days.

My lady of parts
unknown   to arm your legacy
I know you willed only your heart.

89

The rest was merely flesh
and all you had to give.
Only now I can accept
that this last compassion was compatible
with everything else you were, you
who mothered the troubled of this world
but were yourself caught   finally
        too long in the dreaming.

Dichotomized   not only
the poetry of your gentle mind survived
        but somewhere yet
a gentler heart may ache
in some alien breast
and thoughtless fingers still cry
and yesterday, on passing whim,
it could have been your half-remembering eyes
that seemed
        to want
            to speak
                to me.

Helen Norris

Retired from the English Department of Huntingdon College, Helen Norris devotes her time to creative writing. A fiction writer as well as a poet, Norris has had two collections of short stories published, *The Christmas Wife* and *Water Into Wine*. Three stories from *The Christmas Wife* appeared in *Prize Stories: The O. Henry Awards*. Her poetry has appeared in *Negative Capability*.

Portrait of Mother and Sorrowing Child

I gather his brokenness,
Having and holding
Wild seatangle
Of shackled dust,
My chin to kneel
On earth-smelling hair.
He is kenneled in me
This moonset hour,
A stillborn child.
We stare together
At desert places,
The edges of cliffs,
The shattered shores,
The wild deep graves
That are filled with night,
The shapes of ice
We had almost forgot.

Brimming with sky and
Garlanded, we walked
With the sickle moon,
Light years ago.

Window

That summer we took down the screens
To paint the house a bridal white
And day went down before we'd put them back.
In bed we drank the newly painted
Walls like wine. Sea-washed they were,
A bone-sweet shell to latch us in
And seal us up with singing dark.

The window was a rift in the teeming night.
The roaming moon invaded us. The birds
Flew in and beat their wings against its
Mirrored shimmer in our glass and nested
Muttering in the gloom above the door.
Our faces brushed with moth, our minds
Grew heavy with the chirring of the crickets
Round our bed. The ivy we had loosened
From the bricks swept past the sill.
We felt root fingers touch our throats
Binding breath and greening us to sleep . . .

But first we loved. The stars came in
And signed us with their silver. Fireflies
Were weaving our embrace. Moving leaves
Were crowning us with summer. We were
Made new like all the house around us.
First time to love, first time to sleep . . .

For we had slipped beyond the shell gate.
We were deep in Eden garden.
Deep and rich the scent of moon.

Summerscape

Today the town is laced
With sea: foam and sand
Vapor, tower, liquid air
And sea wall have embraced
Like weeping lovers. The land
Itself is blurred like memories.
We watch the mist erase
Its lines . . . its time.
The huddled island houses
Will dissolve without a trace
And drift from us into
A summer we had cast
Away. Perhaps they have
Not even come to pass
Like light from distant stars
Long dead and past
That travels toward a sea-dream
Summer a century from now

And reaches it when we are grown
Too dry, our bodies too precise
To claim it for our own.

Do Beasts Hear Music . . .

Do beasts hear music
When we see them
Lowing in the field,
Their heads pulled skyward
And their full necks curved
And yearning toward the sun,
Their hooves deep planted in
The moving grass like stones?

Beneath the blue they chew
In loving rhythm. Their throats
Will swell and hunger for
Antiphonal communion
Till they trumpet forth.
Is it a bestial urge
To join with crows among
The canebrakes, thrushes calling
From the willows, grasses
Whispering 'round their hooves—
To sing the world together,
Hymn division into
Wholeness? That and more.
Their eyes are human-kind
And dreaming of the spheres.

Alan Perlis

Although a native of Boston, Massachusetts, Alan Perlis has lived for more than a dozen years in Birmingham, Alabama, where he is professor of English at the University of Alabama at Birmingham. He has written books on Wallace Stevens, James Joyce, and George Eliot. *Skin Songs*, a collection of his poetry, was published by Thunder City Press.

Alabama Is a State of Mind

It's man against the ants:
the fattest termites north of Nogales,
oily and stuffed as bulls,
gobbing tunnels in the piling of our houses
intricate as veins and spacious as a Roman bath.
Listen in the warm night
when honeysuckle throbs its scent away.
You can hear Alabama boring and chewing
across the Appalachians.
And when luna moths,
teased by false light,
beat their viola wings
on our windows,
lovers and fanatics leap from cliffs;
cars, their radios seeping o promise me
into the night,
plunge headlong together,
fireball down Red Mountain gap.

At 1:00 a.m. a phone rings;
a light sprays through the woods;
a voice whines: "I only wanted to hear another voice;
speak to me."
The line clicks shut;
the light pinpoints away;
junebugs fall from the windows,
whir their life away upon their backs.
Alabama is a crosseyed child
mooning in upon itself,
growing mad on its own fecundity.
Wisteria grows so thick on trees
it chokes them, then it burns away
to tissue skeletons in raw May sun;
fire ants pare carcasses to bone,

then flute the bones
and spool their chorus all night long.
Everyone dreams of falling off the world,
falling away, wriggling from her mandible grip
to sleep, simply to sleep.

Showing Off

for Harry Perlis, 1901-1985

The evening after his father's funeral
he sits with his family
to leaf through photographs.
The sandy-haired boy in sailor suit
posing by the Volga is his grandfather,
primped and brushed to celebrate Czar Nicholas
who ten years later will impress him
in the army. A group of people
picnic in the background,
squinting into sunlight, bees swarming
about bottlenecks, cheese running
on big loaves of bread. They are
great-grandparents, imaging an America
of golden wheat and ships with soaring spars
they'll never see. They recline
on one arm, smiling proudly at their son
who is already planning an escape
and dreams about the cattle
he will one day fatten
somewhere West of uniforms and shuls.

In another picture his grandmother,
still alive at ninety-nine, is flaxen,
blue-eyed, gurgling, propped
upon a pillow, staring at a blackbox
that leaves the mote of its shutter snap
in her eye. She will depart from Russia
when she's nine and wind up
in Connecticut, a crinolined valedictorian
at sixteen, a baker of breads,
a poultry plucker, maker of blintzes.

In infant photographs his father,

first of a family to be born in America,
in the natal year of the century,
has great hands, plump and grasping,
a gaze as silent as his death,
and is surrounded by those huge
floral drapes of studios.
When turned, the pictures of his father
form a forty-five year kinescope of dancing:
war—affluence and huge black cars—poverty
and war again; bars, beaches
where fat men smoke cigars and bet on pinochle,
Packards, skinny kids with alfalfa freckles,
sailor suits, zoot-suits and salutes.
His father, a portly businessman
with a Chesterfield stuck in his mouth,
has a son during the second war,
names him after Abraham,
has him bar-mitzvahed
on the eve of Eisenhower's second term.
The son's wife is by his side,
newcomer to a family that offers her
more past than she can possibly take in.
A baby is in his lap—the blonde,
blue-eyed and chubby pride
of this dark, mustachioed man.
Everyone remarks that the wife,
Scotch-Irish, golden-haired,
resembles his grandmother,
the last shiksah-looking
member of the family, who refused
to see her dying son-in-law.
For the first time he knows why—
he was of a different century
from the one she shrivels back to,
her watery eyes mirrors
in which photographs turn
like pages in the holy books.

The baby is the family's first
not to know each grandparent.
Its father cries,
not for his father or himself
or for his grandmother, but for his son
whom he suddenly needs so badly,
stunned to love something

96

as fragile and diaphanous as baby flesh,
someone he has photographed over and over
and shows off to the funeral guests.

Morton D. Prouty, Jr.

Morton D. Prouty, Jr., Alabama's 1987-91 Poet Laureate, has had six collections of poetry published, including *The Edge of Time* in 1988. A resident of Florence, Alabama, he is a corporate officer with AlaTenn Resources, Inc.

Scattered Stones

There is something about a ruin
that will not let the stones be content with their silence,
for they have heard
the long outcrying of life and the whispered secret,
and they have listened
unto the sound of prayers said in their presence.

I never look on a ruin
except I remember
that scattered stones are not the same
as stones which have never been gathered.

When April Turned Her Left Cheek Toward the North

I felt the south wind
caress my cheek. I saw
roses. I kissed
April on the lips
and drew her toward me.

Ice
sharpened the thorns
that pierced my fingers.

Thomas Rabbitt

Since coming to Alabama in 1972, Thomas Rabbitt, a native of Hyde Park, New York, has directed the University of Alabama's M.F.A. Program. His first collection of poetry, *Exile*, won the United States Award of the International Poetry Forum. His second collection, *The Booth Interstate*, was nominated for a Pulitzer Prize. Carnegie Mellon University Press published his latest collection, *The Abandoned Country*.

Staying on Alone

I am pretending to be old, that you
Aren't dead. Today your family has come
To take your clothes and books back home.
I ask them leave me you. They say
It is warm in Paris, it is cold, it snows,
Oui, non. They smile like bankers.
It is warm. They count your shoes.

Tell me the world is not ourselves.
It is a small garden where potatoes grow.
Or tell me it is like the race course
In the woods. Tell me.
I can believe that we are both.

Here in the woods of Boulogne faces crop
Out of trees. For one, yours. You are grey,
What you must look like now,
Skin like old food, dead and left
Underground where it will keep.

They have taken down your paintings,
Left my walls, left me old bright spaces
Like a chessboard. Time tells, time plays.
When I go out I see in the trees of Boulogne
My lifetime. I see your faces
Smiling out of the bark. The touch is grey.
I feel dead, that all I am is waiting.

The Monday Before Thanksgiving

The swamped sun setting behind the water oaks
Shoots fire across my pasture and my pond,
Past barn and house, and across the road
Into the burnished butterfly pines. Narrow your lids
And your last hopes. All these Alabama trees
Light up like Maine. *Alabama: State of Mind.*
What's wrong is the tragedy of light, the fire
Shot flat through trees in that last flash
We see before the great mad bombs must take us out.
The sun hisses and slips like shit into the swamp.
This morning I promised myself I'd transplant
The roses some fool planted where the cows cross
Coming home. For two years I've waited for his irony
To drop in on me like light from a far off star.
What returns is the realtor carried back by her own
Prismatic sonic booms: dwarf yellow, giant red,
And these, the golden white they call moon sun.
What a card! And I without the courage to see them
For what they are, the names of trash. I prune them
Down to stumps. I dig in. I uproot. I do my best
To spare the fine hairs of the roots, the dark webs
More felt than seen in the small light I have left.
Around me the livestock clamor to be fed. The dogs
Chase pullets up and down the lot. One horse will not
Stop striking his shod forefoot against the metal gate,
The clang insistent as a bell. A pair of turkey hens,
Two bronze phoenixes done up in sunset kerosene,
Roost like vultures on the rattling metal gate.
Christmas and Thanksgiving are their cooking names,
Talismans against the cowardice I cannot face.
The horse will not stop striking time against the gate.
From the weedy dam the ducks and geese peer down
And the dogs chase one doomed hen across the pasture,
Through barbed wire and off into the swamp.
Their cries grow faint and the sun goes out like that,
Like danger fading, the air going cooler and cooler.
The roots of the roses do not easily let go; the thorns
Hold back from the night the last of the day's heat.
You dig like that—with ungloved fingers deep
Into the dirt until what you feel is quiet and dark,
Until what you feel is finally cold.

For Those Who Will Live Forever

The law said Dale Booth died of falling.
Some nights Dell Booth sits at home and drinks.
His wife talks on. Dell sits and stares
Through the thin pane of his picture window
Down through the burned pines to the highway.
He thinks that everyone is moving away.
The glass shakes. Dale Booth died at two,
Aged two, at two in the morning, of falling
When Dell, falling, could not bear the screaming
And pulled the blocks from beneath his son's end
Of their mobile home. Some nights, late, Dell thinks
He hears a child calling from the tall goldenrod
Near the roadway. *Sorry. Sorry.* But it is only
A possum or dog some car has killed.

Tortoise

I guess today's another day among the days
When nothing ever happens well,
Another afternoon lost drinking, rocker
Jammed against the front porch wall.
Spring. And it has just stopped raining. Two boys
Come loping up the muddy road.
The boys decide to stop, unload their load,
A turtle on the porch for me to praise,
Which I do, I do, box turtle, which they say
They found abandoned and alone
And nearly dead beside the road
And will I let them put it in my pond.
I will. I do. And when, just like a stone,
It sinks and does not rise again, I say,
Don't worry, turtles always sink this way.
The boys spend hours watching and I sit back
To drink my beer. The ducks raise hell. The sun
Setting lights up the water while the boys
Gaze out over the pond. They shake their heads
And take this as their loss. Yes, I can lie.
Yes, I will tell them what I do not know.

101

September 1, 1983

In memory of KAL flight 007

Like a rhyme told on toes the pigs in the bed
Of the passing truck are off. *We're off!*
And their eyes aren't really mirrors,
Their snouts snuffling through the bars don't speak.
The beautiful world hasn't failed them once again.
Look! The sunset opens. Bright light falls out
Of the sky. Let's gather up and save the merely dead.
Let's make the headlines fit the neighbor's pigs.

Everyone knows that this is a killer road.
But I can't tell the boy. His dead dog is load
Enough. *Son,* I say, *can I carry you home?*
He looks up until I'm through.
Trouble is, the goldenrod's too high, the poke
Weed berries are just too purple to believe.
His dog is really dead. It's my house, my road,
My beery grief. *Believe me, boy, I grieve.*

Being drunk is easy. I look up from the porch,
Up from my beer. The sky is so doomed, so rare
I want a photograph, so blue I want to swim
Out of my sticky bones. At last, tonight, it's clear
What I expect from my life. Up through the gate the lurch
Of my neighbor's truck. Back from the market
The squeal of the saved pigs. Out of the terrible scream
The smiles. This, this, this is what I have done.

Margaret Renkl

Margaret Renkl, a native of Andalusia, Alabama, studied creative writing with James Dickey while attending the University of South Carolina. Her poems have appeared in numerous publications, including *Shenandoah, Kentucky Poetry Review, Southern Poetry Review, Texas Review,* and *From the Green Horseshoe: Poems by James Dickey's Students.*

The Way In

Always there are windows, the house
divided into openings, as if for light
all glass is pure enough and sight is easy;
and always I am here inside: wanting

something somewhere else, and light.
Ivy in clay pots, a bowl of waxy apples,
that dark frame hanging crooked on the wall,
the rounded backs of chairs:

all demand my hands, and everything
so wholly known pulls hard against the need
to rise to light more huge and new
than this dark room can hold or I can see:

and yet to hold requires a looking
through: begins in separation: before
the world my own dark eyes, a dusty
window: the tree, the leaf, the smallest

spray of crocus needles barely breaking
ground: all somehow needed now
for passage, allowing movement only
in the mind and deep inside the eye:

not in the hand, not in the hard arched
foot, not in the restless heaviness
of rooms, of everything that has known
my hand. Stillness becomes arrival.

And what has come belongs to me, entering
my eyes: the leaf is mine, the brightest
needle: slick and tightened, yielding green
to find the hand, the quiet fingers; sounding

103

in the veins and gone past every kind
of sight, never to be reached
through windows, swollen past the ways
of human eyes, of animal understanding.

All those heavy things turn light and lift
themselves beyond my hands, will sense
the sounding in my veins and pass through,
entering the heart and beating there in leaves.

In Grace

Holding still enough to breathe
is what we learn in August
from cats stretched flat
beneath the brown azaleas,
from cats and elderly women
closed inside their shuttered houses,
even from songbirds deep
in the hearts of shadowless
trees. The spinning world slows

to plague us at noon, to drive
us to rooms that should be dark
behind blinds but can never be
anything but utterly open

to what might pass for air,
drive us, naked, to our naked bed,
air our only blanket now, losing
cover forever from our language,
relying on a miracle of water
to fill its place, to fall,
even in the unbearable noon.

A room leafs out
and greens, pale grasses
spring up from boards—
corners fill, soften
with vines, and the muffled
sounds of colored birds
lift the vacancy of silence.

We feel it fall
over the dust on our skin,
fill our eyes and our hands,
slide across the flat bones
of our faces, and into our mouths,

making of us a covenant in summer,
what only those who love can offer:
in seasons of drought, rain.

The Swarming

The ants have turned the fence
to breathing,
shaped dull metal into foil
light-shaken,
made the steady chain shiver:
all bodies
silking its surface, drying
new wings in the sun.

Twining and turning to silver,
links come to light,
held separate and moving apart,
blended together,
divided and balanced;
each link betraying a queen.

I have waited since childhood
in darkness.
The earth has shifted for me,
every grain moved
for my growing, my new shape,
for what dry light
can make of wings, perfect and wet,
taking on air.

Bonnie Roberts

Born in Florence, Alabama, Bonnie Roberts has been a resident of Huntsville, Alabama, for many years. She has read her poetry throughout the United States and in Europe, and her work has appeared in more than fifty publications, including *Piedmont Literary Review, Permafrost, Encore, San Fernando Poetry Journal, Amelia, Berkeley Poets Cooperative, Poetry Australia,* and *The Yellow Butterfly.*

Mother Taught Me I Was Beautiful

Beauty was a Fifth Avenue commodity,
the slick of a chiseled nose on Vogue or
the rapiered teeth of young men selling designer jeans.
At its very noblest, it was an intellectual thing,
a cold statue above the overly-polished floors
of the Louvre.
I never connected beauty with nature
or with me.

Then in my thirty-fourth year,
I discovered the large veins
rising
on the backs of my hands,
running,
blue rivers,
beneath the delicate skin,
disappearing into my body
as underground springs
and artesian wells
of nourishment.
Mother had large veins also
and I remember now how gently and kindly
she touched me with her hands
always hoping to teach her daughter
about the beauty of rivers.

How Aliens Survive on This Planet
(Why Mother and I Garden)

Mother was a beautiful earthling,
planting on the farm
and the green alien came in a silver ship and
looked down upon her and spread his martian seed
in the tube rose, mint and wild grape of evening air
and she walked the furrows laughing
and wet her toes in the back door faucet,
and thus conceived me,
mud and water body, alien soul.
Sometimes we long for my father to return in his ship
and search for him in the whirling orbs of the spring sky
and Mother and I, by the moon, plant tomatoes, potatoes and peas,
harvesting more and more green each summer,
signaling.

Take Me Down That Row One More Time, Green-Eyed Boy

I always have plenty of green for you, cousin,
the green silk corn shucks of our childhood
piling us in Uncle's harvest wagon up to the moon
or your mama's peas and fried green tomatoes
tasting like hues of shade
beneath the fence-line tree
on the cotton picker's sack
when the noon bell rang.
And on days when work was done,
we sat on the fat pond moss of our playhouse rug
or ran through the tall meadow grass,
hiding, rolling, planning in the earth,
itching, powerful with chiggers, to be grown,
silly things,
and the summer blades cut our faces,
without pain.
In those days, sweet cuz,
even blood
ran green.

Charles B. Rodning

Charles B. Rodning, Minnesotan by birth, lives in Mobile, Alabama, where he is an associate professor in the Department of Surgery and Anatomy at the University of South Alabama's College of Medicine. His poetry appears in more than fifty publications, including *The Red Pagoda, Frogpond, Poetry Nippon, Amelia, Suwannee Press*, and *The Cambridge Collection*. His two newest books are *Elan Vital: A Chapbook of Oriental Poetry and Sumi-e Painting* and *Wode and Ston: A Collecte of Poetry in the Oriental Tradition*.

Haiku Sequence

dripping woods
the whispering
of a nightingale

white chrysanthemums
on a gravestone -
fluttering black moth

wind-swept cloudy beach -
the sting
of salt rain

sunlight turns
mill wheel shadows
on a frozen stream

far from home -
blossoms in a plum tree
how they wave

deep ruts
narrow road
turning back

walking slowly
    under wisps of spanish moss -
crunching acorns

a red mitten
    dangling from the rope -
empty swing

Dennis Sampson

Although a native of Pierre, South Dakota, Dennis Sampson has lived in Tuscaloosa, Alabama, for the past decade and has worked as a staff member at Shelton State Community College. *The Double Genesis*, a collection of his poetry, was published in 1985 by Story Line Press and was selected by the National Endowment for the Arts for display at the Frankfurt, Germany, Bookfair. Several magazines have published his poems, including *The Hudson Review*, *Ploughshares*, *The Ohio Review*, *The South Dakota Review*, and *The Black Warrior Review*.

Prayer

I would like to sprawl in fury over the earth,
to purify the vile with a cast of my hand
and lie down in the pasture like light,
the grasses moving and broad
under my tremendous belly.
I would like to walk out of my body,
become another thing more muscular,
a huge mare brooding, solitary and brown,
beneath vast sky, her last life flying behind her,
becoming wind exploring with interest the winter trees.
I would like to glide beside these
high stacks of wood, trailing a finger
along the lip of a trough,
feeling the incalculable power of the land.

Sadness, That's the Word

Some blessedness to make it through the day,
a touch along my wrists to trace my veins,
my daughter, stopping to explain which streaks
deliver, which receive. Shocking, this quick caress
across my wrist, until, trembling, I had to grab
her hand. Gently, my fingers embracing the back
of her hand, she broke my grip, pulling me close
to clutch and lightly kiss me on the nose.

Whirling suddenly away from me, she seemed
pleased, while I, wondering what I must have really felt,

watched an ivy climbing into branches
of a nearby tree. Beyond, the window of a kitchen
began to shine. Not long ago the face
of a father shone, in a window such as this. Dazed
and gazing backward of the heart, he stayed
like that for the longest time. And then, by God,

he went away. Sadness, that's the word
to describe my heart, feeling Gloria's finger
on my wrist, my father, away and strange to me,
whom I keep finding to follow back to life.

The Secret Tree

What a mysterious tree,
out of the wind because down in the valley.
It looks mesmerized for life. We
could dazzle our friends by climbing it.
We could cut it down. Can't
you imagine the billowing dust?

Ariel must hide there—curious specter—
always on the opposite side of where we are.
Like a disciple, it needs its privacy.
Lacking apples, it must wonder
Will we ever see Eden again,
a garden exploding around us, gorgeous with poppies?

Put the tree in a class by itself.
Think how it suffers, alone.
I want my sadness to be big, like the tree's.
See how it stands at the back of the mind,
remembering as we remember Eve?
God gave everyone an apple. We gobbled it up.

The Turtle

I had immediate compassion
for the turtle—it was so solemn when I came upon it
in the field. It gazed at me
even at this distance
with bitter, bitter eyes, contracting its fleshy neck

when I stepped slowly forward to probe and tease it
with a stick
to see what it might do,
everything withdrawn in an instant. Yet it
was quite impatient to be on its grueling way, in search of water,

so, after despising me for a little while
(yet it was no gloomier than before)
protruded its ugly head and thrust away, so serious,
wretched, like a murderer, splattered all over with mud.

And I followed it, belittling its slowness, I let it bitch,
impeding its progression across the field by wedging
a stalk between its beak—it shrunk back, and I rocked it over.
I thought: You are the opposite of bird. You hate the earth.

Here then, the turtle, comforted by no one—
unable to embrace, to plead, preferring the interminable silence
to the screech of birds—the stars, which you do
not see, do not exist for you; nevertheless, you meditate,

unlike a lover, upon the context of your brittle soul,
bitterly. Like a hermit, you reek of urine,
and are humorless—which makes me want to say
Turtle, if you were to appear to me as human

I would name you Brutus, and send you away
to brood and ruminate forever in a private room,
grouchy, overweight—your soul gone sour as your socks.
But wait. Wronged, intimidated by sticks, by birth-right cursed

to suffer the indignity of being turtle, you wander
over the stubble field; your hiss is justified, is right—
I see it in your eyes. And while I look
at you now, at the mythological strangeness of your belly,
butter colored, the scripture written there

comes clear to me—that you are unknowable to me
as to yourself, yet truth abides in you, evanescent
as a dragonfly. If only I, you, could find it
we might meet, without suspicion, in the stubble field,

which is ridiculous, I know. And so I roll you over
and wait, some ways off, to let you pass
into the shadow beside the pool.

Sonia Sanchez

Born in Birmingham, Alabama, Sonia Sanchez has lectured on poetry and read her poems at more than 500 universities and colleges in America, Cuba, Australia, the Caribbean, Nicaragua, Norway, Canada, and the People's Republic of China. She is the author of thirteen books, including *Homecoming*, *We a BaddDDD People*, *Love Poems*, *Homegirls and Handgrenades*, and *Under a Soprano Sky*. She lives in Philadelphia, Pennsylvania, where she is Presidential Fellow and Professor of English at Temple University.

From a Black Feminist Conference
Reflections on Margaret Walker: Poet

chicago/october 1977/saturday afternoon/margaret walker walks her red clay mississippi walk into a room of feminists. a strong gust of a woman. raining warm honeysuckle kisses and smiles. and i fold myself into her and hear a primordial black song sailing down the guinea coast.

her face. ordained with lines. confesses poems. halleluyas. choruses. she turns leans her crane like neck on the edge of the world, emphasizing us. in this hotel/village/room. heavy with women. our names become known to us.

there is an echo about her. of black people rhyming. of a woman celebrating herself and a people. words ripen on her mouth like pomegranates. this pecan/color/woman. short limbed with lightning. and i swallow her whole as she pulls herself up from youth, shaking off those early chicago years where she and wright and others turned a chicago desert into a well spring of words.

eyes. brilliant/southern eyes torpedoing the room with sun. eyes/dressed like a woman. seeing thru riddles. offering asylum from ghosts.

she stands over centuries as she talks. hands on waist. a feminine memory washed up from another shore. she opens her coat. a light colored blouse dances against dark breasts. her words carved from ancestral widows rain children and the room contracts with color.

her voice turns the afternoon brown. this black woman poet. removing false veils, baptizes us with syllables. woman words. entering and leaving at will:

114

Let a new earth rise. Let another world be born. Let a bloody peace be written in the sky. Let a second generation full of courage issue forth; let a people loving freedom come to growth. Let a beauty full of healing and a strength of final clenching be the pulsing in our spirits and our blood. Let the martial songs be written, let the dirges disappear. Let a race of men now rise and take control.*

walking back to my room, i listen to the afternoon. play it again and again. scatter myself over evening walls and passageways wet with her footprints. in my room i collect papers. breasts. and listen to our mothers hummmmming

*For My People by Margaret Walker

words
(for mr. and mrs. rinaldi)

i saw death
   today
and didn't know what
to do with it.
   obscene/
      yellowish/
         death
lounging on a pennsylvania
farm.
   i screamed at death
      today
but my words ran down
against autumn's
   fast pace.
   i know nothing
of here/
   after songs
      of space/filled with souls.
i know only
   that children bloom
      and fade like
         flowers
and that death is a six
o'clock door
   forever changing time.

115

On Passing thru Morgantown, Pa.

i saw you
vincent van
gogh perched
on those pennsylvania
cornfields communing
amid secret black
bird societies. yes.
i'm sure that was
you exploding your
fantastic delirium
while in the
distance
red indian
hills beckoned.

under a soprano sky

    1.

once i lived on pillars in a green house
boarded by lilacs that rocked voices into weeds.
i bled an owl's blood
shredding the grass until i
rocked in a choir of worms.
obscene with hands, i wooed the world
with thumbs
               while yo-yos hummed.
was it an unborn lacquer i peeled?
the woods, tall as waves, sang in mixed
tongues that loosened the scalp
and my bones wrapped in white dust
returned to echo in my thighs.

i heard a pulse wandering somewhere
on vague embankments.
O are my hands breathing? I cannot smell the nerves.
i saw the sun
ripening green stones for fields.
O have my eyes run down? i cannot taste my birth.

2.

now as i move, mouth quivering with silks
my skin runs soft with eyes.
descending into my legs, i follow obscure birds
purchasing orthopedic wings.
the air is late this summer.

i peel the spine and flood
the earth with adolescence.
O who will pump these breasts? I cannot waltz my tongue.

under a soprano sky, a woman sings,
lovely as chandeliers.

A Poem for Jesse

your face like
summer lightning
gets caught in my voice
and i draw you up from
deep rivers
taste your face of a
thousand names
see you smile
a new season
hear your voice
a wild sea pausing in the wind.

Haiku

we are sudden stars
you and i exploding in
our blue black skins

Sue Scalf

Sue Scalf, a native of Barbourville, Kentucky, has lived in Alabama for more than two decades. Her poems have appeared in *Scrod I*, *Tennessee Voices*, *Encore*, *Voices International*, *The Sampler*, and *The Southern Review*, and Troy State University has published a collection of her poetry, *Devil's Wine*. She teaches English at Troy State University at Montgomery.

The Waiting Room

There you sit, gentle anachronism in a chrome and vinyl chair.
Eight floor tiles between us span a chasm.
Hating to stare, I fidget, look around the room,
but I am drawn to you,
drawn to your purple sun-bonnet.
Do you know we have been to the moon?
Crossed ankles encased in thick stockings
swollen above old lady comforts,
arthritic hands rest palms upward.
They are carved wooden flowers.
Your hooded eyes are calm.
And upon your head that burning bonnet, that glowing bonnet,
a pivot of color in a colorless room.
Archetype, earth mother,
my intellect strings words my heart ignores.
In this air-conditioned tomb
you are a summary of summers past,
redolent of hollyhocks and zinnias,
sweet mint and sassafras.
I snub out my Virginia Slim
and observe my nervous hands.
They are naked, plastic flowers.
And I am tired.
I ache to lay my head upon your ample breast.
How can I live in this world
when there are no purple bonnets left?
The nurse calls my name and a number,
assigning me my cubicle.

Absolution

Legs apart, feet firmly in the sand,
I stand and face the sea,
and I open like a window
the wind blows through.
Far away, a dipping gull genuflects
in fading light.
The waves swell and throb a Gregorian chant,
recede as small shells click like beads,
and I open like a window
the wind blows through.
A star or two flicker faintly as votive candles
or the the heart of a sanctuary light;
sea spray tastes of tears,
but lighter, cleaner.
Mea culpa, mea culpa,
dark, heavy words have no place here.
Father, it has taken so many years,
but I have learned to love myself a little.
A thin moon appears.
And I am a window the wind blows through.

Charles Scott

A native of Fort Payne, Alabama, Charles Scott has traveled to Yugoslavia on
an NEH grant to interview Eastern European poets. A chapbook of his poetry,
The River Is Laughing, was published in 1987, and his work has appeared in
several magazines, including *Poetry Miscellany* and *The Sequoyah Review*.
He is currently studying under a Mitchell Fellowship at the University of
Houston.

Autobiography from Down the Hall

I can tell it in two quick breaths.
Two months to the day before her marriage,
my mother positioned a red peony
in her hair; she was stretched in mid-field
beneath the tobacco's tangy smell, the milkweed
feathers clouding the sky. And my father's fingers
freshly washed in well water, wrote a sentence
from her knee heading to thigh, a sentence
he whispered to the peony, that said,
in so many words, the secret to desire
is to not quite see. Not quite nine months
later with the tobacco just off the drying
racks, I was no more a secret, the black
cloud of my hair rushing out slick
as sweat, slick as my father's virgin fingers.

This my father wanted to tell me the summer
he died, but the stroke had carried with it
most of his body, more of his words. What he had
left were his eyes, he'd turn his eyes
toward the river where the wind was making
many ripples like thousands of snakes. What becomes
of memory when there are no more words?
A faint tinge to the mind? Glimmer
of image—a path to fallow fields,
the silence of fallen seeds, hands held in water?

My father practiced law, the sale
of land, the luck of divorcees. *Which color
corresponds to Venezuela?* my mother, the geography
teacher, asked me. As a kid, I couldn't care
less. I specialized in disease: Chicken Pox,
Measles, tooth decay, even typhus. By the time

I grew up, my body had nothing left
to give. Nor did my mother and father.

But look at what I have now: a pension, good clean
rooms, a view of the river, a young lady who brings
bread, candy, and flowers in a cut-glass carafe.
And that's all I need, really all. The days I just
shuffle away like a not too good hand of cards,
and the snakes, come out on the porch and
look, the snakes I still see quite clearly,
rippling the cloud-dark waters.

My Brother's Maze

Some things were sure:
The night guard's scream when
Wet leaves reached out of the black
Across his face; or that, if the jungle
Suddenly opened up, whatever
Stood in its place, cattle,
Bamboo, villagers, air, would be
Stamped with bullets and
Counted as enemy killed.

The country up that thin
Branch of the Mekong needed
Weeding out. But the bodies
Bumping past your boat seemed to
Know a stronger command. *We know
Little*, you wrote home, *of our destination*.

There was a pond, since drained
And filled, you and I lobbed rocks into.
I called the splash rings secret blasts.
Once, circling it we found stray pups
Feeling for their mother's milk.
Her nipples kept peeking through, pointed
Against the rainy season's volley of wind.
Then you reached down. You said
It was best, and you carried the pups
To a stone wall and cracked their skulls.

Today, you weave through the maze

121

Left by shattered fragments in your brain.
They say a soldier sees three things
When it hits: plum splotches
Pink confetti, a hand closing in.

Sometimes sitting with you, we imagine again
The ponds, the smell of pine, paddies ripped by rain,
And your eyes trail off to the window,
Beyond that last line of clouds rising
Against the sky, hiding whole battalions
Of geese who, like the words
You hold yourself still to remember,
Drift silently towards an unknown land.

Mushrooms

Floating in the closet light of dawn,
they're the moon remembered many
times over — *Orange Peel, Eyelash, Burn
Cup* — like the little bumps coming to
your skin when you were cold
or scared — *goose flesh of the field.*

At six this morning,
the deadly *Alcohol Angel* spilled
a shadow five times its height and I left
it untouched just as Father left his.
He'd found one wedged upside-down behind
our bathtub; he gave Mother some mean
words and a good slap and my sister
and I could see the sweat beading
down the back of his neck. He was
almost forty, bending over, breath lost to breath.
Then he stroked my mother's arm all the way
back to their bedroom, and my sister
said she could hear him crying.
Grief needs only a handful of dirt to grow.
But these mushrooms, picked, washed now,
and dripping in the window, are past all that.
They take the charred soil the summer fires leave
and make what's needed to live.
So long as there's rain. And what isn't, finally,

a product of decay? And after the past
is rinsed away like so much mud, it's these
few stars that remain, that show the sudden
and exact knowledge a cold spring shower
shows, when seen ticking steadily
towards you across the lawn.

Jim Simmerman

Jim Simmerman, the son of an Air Force sergeant, grew up in Selma, Alabama, during the 70's. His poetry collections include *Home, Bad Weather*, and *Once Out of Nature*, and his poems have appeared in numerous publications, such as *Poetry, Pushcart Prize X, Sonora Review, Laurel Review*, and *The Iowa Review*. He teaches in the writing program at Northern Arizona University in Flagstaff.

Child's Grave, Hale County, Alabama

Someone drove a two-by-four
through the heart of this hard land
that even in a good year
will notch a plow blade worthless,
snap the head off a shovel,
or bow a stubborn back.
He'd have had to steal
the wood from a local mill
or steal, by starlight, across
his landlord's farm, to worry
a fencepost out of its well
and lug it the three miles home.
He'd have had to leave his wife
asleep on a cornshuck mat,
leave his broken brogans
by the stove, to slip outside,
lullaby soft, with the child
bundled in a burlap sack.
What a thing to have to do
on a cold night in December,
1936, alone
but for a raspy wind
and the red, rock-ridden dirt
things come down to in the end.
Whoever it was pounded
this shabby half-cross
into the ground must have toiled
all night to root it so:
five feet buried with the child
for the foot of it that shows.
And as there are no words
carved here, it's likely that
the man was illiterate,
or addled with fatigue,

or wrenched simple-minded
by the one simple fact.
Or else the unscored lumber
driven deep into the land
and the hump of busted rock
spoke too plainly of his grief—
forty years layed by and still
there are no words for this.

Almost Dancing

In this kind of wind
blowing hard from the west—
sloughed off the Pacific
to dust the desert floor,
collecting all that chaff and grit
and whatever else a wind needs
to huff headlong into these mountains—
even the half-dead, lackluster pines
bow a bit from their stiff waists,
begin to dip and sway;
their boughs nodding together
like the heads of drunks
with nowhere to go
between last call and their dark, bolted homes—
the last bars of a two-bit tune
blowing from the jukebox—
almost touching because of the beat,
almost dancing. . . .

I was the kid with two left feet
in a school where most of my classmates
majored in meanness
and the stupefying logarithms of sex.
I held up the wall at the senior prom
while the other kids grooved
and ground their groins
like interchangeable parts
in some competent, well-lubed machine.
Even the chaperones shuffled their feet.
Even the sober, undrinkable punch
shimmied like a little sea.
The band played poorly on secondhand instruments

they'd eventually hock
for bus tickets out of town.
I would have left
if I had known where to go.
I would have danced if anyone had asked me.

How simple it looks out there
from in here: back and forth, to and fro.
Not the old-fashioned boxstep exactly,
but some facile choreography
starting low in the roots
and welling up through the trunk,
branches and twigs of every green
and once-green thing.
Likewise the beer cans dumped by the road
and the stopsign on its one metal leg
stir to the vagrant music of March—
the whole world a dancehall
for whatever moves with ease.
How simple it looks out there,
and yet—
what's here to move me to unlock the door,
unlock my bones some
and take the first step?

What's here to move me back
to the N.C.O. Club in Selma, Alabama—
nineteen-seventy-whatever-it-was—
where I sat with my parents
listening to the Ink Spots,
a band fallen to low-rent gigs
for homesick GI's
and blowzy town-girls no one would marry?
It was the first time we got family drunk
and when the game-legged guitarist
kicked the group into "Maybe,"
that graying, corpulent couple
who'd brought me up
breezed to the center of the empty floor
and fell into each other
like falling in love—
dancing so lightly I held my breath,
afraid they'd blow away.

I'd never seen them move like that—
so many moves I've missed.
So many steps I might have learned
by stepping with my wooden feet
into the fanfare of the world,
to let its music play me green.
Maybe the wind that drums these walls,
frets the glass
and whistles down the chimney pipe
could find me with its restless riffs—
take my breath away I mean—
and lead me from myself.
A lithe wind,
a measureless wind
agog with grace notes of seed and decay,
leading nowhere
I could follow for long,
away. . . .

Fetch

The marrow of it's this:
that night after night I dream
you alive, dream you clawing
up and through the snarl
of spade-looped roots and loam,
through the cairn beneath the pine
in a bower of pines, a wildwood
of pines, beneath a wheeling moon—
shaking from your body
the tattered blanket, shaking
from your throat the collar
of blood—the ball
in your mouth where I left it,
your coat wet where I kissed it—
breaking through underbrush
onto the trail, tracking it back
to the tire-rutted road—
loping now, running now—
your nostrils flared
and full of the world—
ignoring the squirrel,
ignoring the jay, ignoring

the freeway's carrion toll—
night nearly dead as you
bolt for the lane,
up the drive, into the yard—
panting now, breathing now—
racing from door to window to door,
scratching at the screen,
whining at the glass, the ball
in your mouth—oh
wouldn't I shake from this
sweet gnawed dream to rise
and fetch you in
with the light that returns
me day after day,
takes you again and again.

To You in Particular

No, this is no voice
from a fiery bush.
But it's something.
It is the paper boat
an orphan makes
and buries
in someone's yard.
It is the promise
made by starlight
in a story
so old
the words have worn
to a threadbare music
that is faith,
though the promise
is forgotten.
No one wants to talk
about miracles anymore.
No one wants to walk,
alone, through the dark
part of town
and kiss the withered hand
of a drunk who might be
anybody's child,
who might be most
of what is given us

to know of love
and the anguish
of Abraham.
As far as I know
the heart
is a paper boat
burning underground.
As far as I know
the world
is a broken promise,
a story
that doesn't know
how to end itself.
But who can say, really—
if the telling is good,
if the words are clear
and strong—
that it is not the voice
of God
speaking, this once,
like a very lonely man
to you in particular?
The knife is in your hand.

Black Angel

There is a cemetery I walk to
in the stiff breath of autumn,
in the lengthening sequence
of dwindling days, where
the bald knolls and hollows
fold in on one another, hide
one thing from the next:
the yew tree from the crepe myrtle,
the garland from the path,
the hole in the land from
the hole in the heart—
I walk there to hide myself
from myself.

      And still
I come stark halt upon

the monument people call
Black Angel—black as a shadow
in deep water, big as a man;
and I wonder, as some must,
drawn again
into its sunken glare,
who would raise such a memory
to himself, to another,
to break from the grave's
belly of snow and stare
the living down, to say
the dead are dead
and don't come back.

                    Each
night I wrestle my own
black angel, who comes upon me
like a sudden mirror,
so that I can feel the black
wings wrenching my shoulders,
see the black lips broken
by desire, by grief—
neither worse, nor less
than my own—so that
I must wrestle each night
until I am exhausted enough
to wake, to walk back
into the world of things
as they are, one step
and its consequence
after the next.

Louie Skipper

A native of Dothan, Alabama, Louie Skipper lives in Tuscaloosa, Alabama, where he teaches at Shelton State Community College. His poems have appeared in *The Kenyon Review, Poetry Northwest, Southern Poetry Review, The Black Warrior Review, The Reaper*, and elsewhere. A new collection of his work, *Deaths That Travel With the Weather*, is soon to be published.

The Light of the World

To Everette Maddox

1

When Wilbur Jackson took the pitchout
                                        at the Crimson Tide 20
            he rolled
            with the backfield to the short side,

        seemed to hesitate,
        almost drift

before spinning
                    completely around the first man

            who tried to take him,
            began to glide up the sideline

near the Bear
then blew past the Tennessee secondary.

In those nine seconds
                    did not something irreversible occur?

            A slave's grandson's son
            raising seventy thousand indifferent men

        to their feet in a spontaneous roar
        from deep inside their own territory:

it was not
            that the coiled fire hoses of Birmingham

131

filled then with their own emptiness
or that the unmarked and shallow graves

rose
in unrequited light

or that in the passing
of one hundred and eight years

the cast iron chokers and the balls and chains
suddenly lost their grip
on the earth.
Yet did not this man

at nineteen,
across eighty yards that were all white

until he tucked the football under his left arm
and ran

through one long cry of pleasure,
did he not take on something more?

Did he not run, once,
out of his life

to join the invisible together like a prayer,
to be skin

the words themselves had grown?
And for a time

the flesh of the Word was
his flesh.

He stepped out of time
and held it against himself

as though running along the eastern edge of the Holy
past where all life can go

without being made again,
while the earth held close

to his every move under the lights,

132

held pale and blue and glorious,

held to the dead and to the living
in downward drawn and nuclear time.

Was he not,
                leaving everyone twenty yards behind him,

            more
            than a man,

having taken hold of something larger
and entered the form of a world that was not his own

so completely
            it became his possession?

        Was he not in fact for that moment a god?

Vivian Smallwood

Vivian Smallwood was born in Vinegar Bend, Alabama, but has lived most of her life in Chickasaw, Alabama, where she worked as a bank employee. She is the author of two poetry collections, *And Finding No Mouse There* and *Window to the South*, and her poems have appeared in two anthologies, *Contemporary Women Poets of America* and *Southern Poets*.

"I Shall Pretend to Be Sleeping"

I shall pretend to be sleeping, just for a day or two,
While living is still a habit and death is so strange and new.
Propped on my smooth white pillow under the quilted grass
I shall pretend to be dreaming, hoping the dream will pass.

Maybe a little later, after the roses fade
And the earth begins to settle, I shall not be afraid.
Maybe a little later I shall be glad to go
Silently into silence, but just for a day or so
I shall be lonely and frightened, waiting for dawn to break,
Pretending that I am sleeping, wishing that I might wake.

And Finding No Mouse There

There was this bit of dry bone on the sand.
The less-than-human skull which once had housed
A less-than-human brain was empty now
And open to the airs. How dead it was!
How polished by the wind and bleached by sun,
Unroofed, unshuttered, stripped and tenantless,
Impersonal as any stick or stone
I might have kicked in passing.
                                    There it lay,
The relic of a summer barely gone,
And there was I, not quite a relic yet,
Peering into the windows of a mouse
And finding no mouse there. What once had lived
Its tiny life and died its tiny death
Beneath the fragile rafters of this room
Had known its last of self.
                                    I sometimes think

(Perhaps because I have a larger skull)
That we are different, the mouse and I,
That something splendid in me will endure;
And then again, sometimes I am not sure
And lift a troubled hand to touch my head,
Still roofed, still shuttered, still inhabited.

Adam at the Gates

Perhaps it was too soon to stand erect,
To claim dominion over land and sea
And name the beasts and give myself a name.
Perhaps I was not ready, after all,
To bear the strange, new burden of a soul.

Yet who would think a soul could weigh so much?
I pulled it from the green, forbidden bough
And held it in the hollow of my hand,
So small a thing, but heavy even then
And heavier with every passing year.
Perhaps I should have dropped it where I stood
And sought again the safety of the brush,
The dark, accustomed shelter of the wood.

Now at the gates of Eden, looking back,
I see the fields and flowers forever lost,
I hear the lean snake hissing in the weeds,
And in my hand I hold the bitter fruit
I picked too soon and cannot put aside.

R. T. Smith

R. T. Smith was born in Washington, D.C., but for more than a decade he has lived in Alabama and has taught at Auburn University, where he has served as Alumni Writer-in-Residence. He is Associate Editor of *Southern Humanities Review* and the author of nine collections of poetry, including *Banish Misfortune*, published by Livingston University Press. His poem "Harpwing" won the 1986 Eugene W. Field Poetry Prize judged by William Stafford.

North of Spruce Pine

Not a fossil. Rather,
fissures antlered in rock's
sheer wall at roadside.

The small faults jag horns
into the deepest crack
like rivers in a delta

where water joins the sea,
or crown bones a buck
raises from laurel sheen

to catch birth-light, dawn
on a ridge spine. Locked
in the cliff, an image

shimmers through light rain.
I wipe my eyes. What luck
to see myth break to life,

the spiked helmet lifting
with lightning in black
granite. Old thunder is

trembling deep in stone.
At once bright and dark,
a creature wakes, is born

against the literal grain.
Savage, that living rock.
Sweet, that morning storm.

Retreat

A summer without schedules,
without mail, with no wife.
Hardened to loss, I fed windfall
limbs to the hearth nightly.
Days I scavenged the chaparral
or watched aspens shiver as
a northern flicker danced alone
in the cottonwood, feasting
on carpenter ants. A male, I knew,
by his red moustache and black
breast crescent, but today
as shadows waxed, I found the bird
limp beneath a red willow,
blood locking his beak. Soon
I gave him—feather, bone,
blood and still eyes—to the snarl
of knot and resin, then thought
how someday I want, too, to be
taken, when the music has fallen
from me and all light is shaken
to stillness. Now I want flight,
plenty and song before blindness,
then one mourner who will know
me by my colors, who will
preside at my burning
and be willing to change.

Carnival Wheels

We all want the full circle, the rounded
rise and earthward fall, and the riskless
wheel of the carrousel won't do
when we get the urge for new birth.
Even griffins, unicorns, the demonic grins
of painted stallions skewered on oil
fall short when the need for orbit
strikes us behind the eyes, when just past
the candy apple stand, the stripper's
lit runway and the ring toss, the double
circle of light rises, neon sizzling,

its locked seats asway against the night.
And if both zeroes ease at once starward
and toward the world where the barker's cant
blurs the arcade organ's strain,
if the roller coaster's shriek of metal
reminds us how machines can fail, if we grip
the rail and gasp in autumn air to foresee
two seconds of wild flight and death
on the midway, can the edge of fear
spoil all joy? That chilled laughter
when we pause at the peak to see
spectators transformed to dream in a bloom
of dust gives us the first surge
of that birth we worship, and the vertigo
that draws us closer, swinging in mid-air
arrest is everything we dare to savor,
trusting darkness, common science, a man
with hearts tattooed on his arm, and where
one eye should be: a frayed black patch,
in the center a circle and a perfect star.

Harpwing

In the absence of fire, a barn swallow
flew down the dark path, backtracking rumors
of smoke. Bewildered, perhaps fleeing rain,
he emerged from my hearth to fly fast
at the windows and walls, soiling the room
with birdlime and soot, wings printing
his terror like dark notes on a page.

When I entered, I caught his panic.
First: burglar? Then: bat? I switched
on the lamp to find him corner-cowering,
his black feathers damaged by the crashing,
thin muscles trembling. Then caught him,
the frail craft hysterical but still
in my palms, wings stiff as dark harps
mute in the season of silence, of cold.

No way to test his flying, so I set him
on the porch rail, stood back to watch.
Quickly he vanished, a blur of starved

harmony joining night's black chord,
the province of storm-washed stars.
Inside again, I lit dry tinder and saw
flame fly. Light sweetened the room.
A wild music inside me dawned.

Jubilee

Some nights in the summer months
sea creatures crawl up on the beach.
Old folks claim they can predict it.
Science can't tell us a thing.
On the east shore of Mobile Bay
I have seen perch, snapper and flounder
flip like jewels on the sand,
shrimp and manta ray dance
like celebrating natives,
a crab gone mad with something
in his blood he could not name
try to climb a tree,
as if evolution were trying to prove
itself in one crazed migration.
We all ran down to the tide's leavings,
boots on and the blue gigs flashing
barbed tines as if to keep the ocean
from changing its mind about the gift.
We collected the insane bounty
and marveled at the sharpened moon
as cook fires lit up the beach.
So we feasted upon the manna cast
on sand, sang the season,
danced the steps of our ancestors
and slept the sleep of men
who have touched the source of dreams.

James Still

Born in LaFayette, Alabama, James Still now lives and writes in the woodlands of Kentucky. His works include novels, short story collections, and poetry collections, the latest being *The Wolfpen Poems*. His poems have appeared in many magazines, such as *The Atlantic Monthly, The Nation, The Virginia Quarterly Review*, and *The New Republic*. The James Still Fellowship for Advanced Study in Humanities was established in 1980 at the University of Kentucky.

River of Earth

The sea saw it and fled. . . . The
mountains skipped like rams, and the
little hills like lambs.

He drank the bright air into his throat
And cast a glance across the shattered thrust
Of hills: And he knew that of all men who slept,
Who waked suddenly, he least of all could name this thing
That held them here. He least could put the sound
Upon his tongue and build the spoken words
That all might know, might speak themselves, might write
In flowing script for those who come upon this place
In curious search, knowing this land for what it is.

But there are those who learn what is told here
By convolutions of earth, by time, by winds,
The water's wearing and minute shaping of man.
They have struck pages with the large print of knowledge,
The thing laid open, the hills translated.
He least can know of this.

He can but stand
A stranger on familiar slopes and drink the restless air,
Knowing that beneath his feet, beneath his probing eyes
A river of earth flows down the strident centuries.
Hills are but waves cast up to fall again, to rise
Still further down the years.

Men are held here
Within a mighty tide swept onward toward a final sea.

140

Spring

Not all of us were warm, not all of us.
We are winter-lean, our faces are sharp with cold
And there is a smell of wood smoke in our clothes;
Not all of us were warm, though we hugged the fire
Through the long chilled nights.

                               We have come out
Into the sun again, we have untied our knot
Of flesh: We are no thinner than a hound or mare,
Or an unleaved poplar. We have come through
To the grass, to the cows calving in the lot.

Wolfpen Creek

How it was in that place, how light hung in a bright pool
Of air like water, in an eddy of cloud and sky,
I will long remember. I will long recall
The maples blossoming wings, the oaks proud with rule,
The spiders deep in silk, the squirrels fat on mast,
The fields and draws and coves where quail and peewees call.
Earth loved more than any earth, stand firm, hold fast;
Trees burdened with leaf and bird, root deep, grow tall.

Year of the Pigeons

In the year of the passenger pigeons
They came in a darkening flood, and the valley of Troublesome
Was heavy with sound. The soft gutturals of their cooing
Were harrows that raked the air and drowned the locusts' thighs.
They came with a cloud of wings that thundered down the hills
And broke the forest with their weight of flesh. Here fell
A snow of dung, here oak and lynn were shaggy with their nests;
Here field and wood, the grain and stalk lost in a feathered hell.

The hollows of Troublesome Creek were glutted with pigeons.
They blew like wind through the trees, and the shuck-dry leaves
Flew from their scratching on the molding floor.
These were no crows flapping above a cornfield:

This was a fire that ran through patch and brush
Eating the milky nubbins, the tender shoots,
The leaf-hoppers, the cankerworms, and maggots of crane-flies
At the grass roots.

The red agate of the pigeons' eyes was the color of death—
Death quiet upon a nest, death feeding her curious milk
From bulging crop, death hovering over pin-feathered squab
With whole-eyed glance upon an infertile egg
On twig-lined shelf: the male warming the oval bulb
Between his legs, squatting with drooping wings;
The female taking her turn upon this stubborn fruit
Of their mating. Death was the silence in the stricken yolk
Turning a living semblance to the trusting breast;
Death running with blood-red feet, with wind-bright eyes
Where wing is interleaved with wing and nest with nest.

Heritage

I shall not leave these prisoning hills
Though they topple their barren heads to level earth
And the forests slide uprooted out of the sky.
Though the waters of Troublesome, of Trace Fork,
Of Sand Lick rise in a single body to glean the valleys,
To drown lush pennyroyal, to unravel rail fences;
Though the sun-ball breaks the ridges into dust
And burns its strength into the blistered rock
I cannot leave. I cannot go away.

Being of these hills, being one with the fox
Stealing into the shadows, one with the new-born foal,
The lumbering ox drawing green beech logs to mill,
One with the destined feet of man climbing and descending,
And one with death rising to bloom again, I cannot go.
Being of these hills I cannot pass beyond.

Patricia Storace

A native of Mobile, Alabama, Patricia Storace has read her work in the Academy of American Poets' "New Voices" series in 1989. Her first book of poetry, *Heredity*, published in 1987 by Beacon Press, won the first annual Barnard New Women Poets Prize. Her poems have appeared in *The New Yorker*, *The New York Times Review of Books*, *The Agni Review*, *Harper's*, *The Paris Review*, *Parnassus*, and elsewhere.

Varieties of Religious Experience

God wants us on our hands and knees.
So, at the right moment in the service,
we drop to the same level, hedges
pruned to equal height.
A woman near me settles into prayer—
a safe return to a well-lit house,
where nothing has been tampered with
and doors are firmly locked against intruders.
I envy her, this rose of prayer,
skirts rippling on the bench with faith,
carrying this Sunday's texts like dew,
neck curved less in submission
than in confidence, needing no more proof
than the unborn generations beneath her dress.
Her husband falls sharply to his knees beside her,
a soldier in a dugout, worshiping a different God
of deadly marksmanship, psalms riddling
his thoughts like snipers' bullets.
A few won't kneel, the diehard democrats
upright in their pews, polite but absolute
in the belief a man's as good as any king.
A grandfather mutters in the corner,
rocking in the cradle of his wish.
A housewife thumps down like dirty laundry
brought here for a scouring.
Myself, I tend to crouch and peer
in the classic posture of intent search,
bent, abject toward the missing object—
contact lens, wedding band, lost subway fare
the gritty pavement threatens to digest—
without which I cannot go home.

Translations from the American

VIII.

A la Mode

Lady, no one is sufficient master yet
of heart's sad craftsmanship, to forget
your opalescent skin, your drifts of brilliant hair—
we suffer you less in losing than in vigil,
watching you living the same way you began
in your silken time, your white height pliant as a shawl.
But now this raised embroidery of ferns unravels
and the glimmering unbalanced fringe shows tears
and too many years of wrapping any shoulders,
anatomied by any insistent airs,
undone by any fingering hands.

Song of Salt and Pepper

Dinner twins,
who remind us that nothing
we know of remains uncoupled or
unparalleled, you revolve from hand to hand,
place to place, like seasons circling
each other in different hemispheres,
converging and married on our evening plates.
One of you, the center of the sea and tears,
reminds us that there is no food
we eat without a bitterness,
that pleasure stings and is
endured like pain;
your mate burns our food and blisters
our mouths, buries in our meat
its devouring flavor, a carnivore
like us, feeding in darkness and in heat.
May the two of you remain in nightly wedding,
teaching us an equal taste for dark and light,
Salt spraying white upon our meal like day,
Pepper grinding black its accompanying night.

The Public Library Stairs

I.

Outside, everything is speaking at once—
a swamp steams with voices,
each creature set to its own tune,
in its own timbre singing the sentence of itself.
A shaggy-textured or smooth-shaven bark
tells what it knows of its tree.
Each fallen leaf with passion repeats
what it has learned of titi or swamp pine.
The tangled vines of the growing world
want witnesses, and clutch at us
to make us stay for one more minute of their story.

II.

Indoors, the world is motionless, and patient.
A mirror gives itself like a saint,
too humble to tell us who its parents are;
its answers translated into our tongue,
with inanimate honesty, tell us what we are.
In this cool hall, the marble floors endure us,
they carry our echoes faithfully,
those mysterious flora our feet plant here,
which will not take root, but open once and die.

III.

Businessmen in suits make a ladder of the stairs,
each step deliberate as a signature,
while old women make decisions at every step;
they hesitate, then standing on the precipice, drop
past couples, walking as steady as a heartbeat,
taking the stairs with a single strong sound,
even when the concrete brims suddenly with children,
foaming and flowing up and down,
plunging past like waters breaking from a dam.

First Love

When you are tuning my body with your eyes,
it seems the dead wouldn't need bodies
to stay alive, it's a strange surprise
that anyone living will ever die,
and all the words for our hopes of peace,
of love, of truth, are wordlessly the color of your eyes,
changing like seasons in the light of mine.
When I move to the chorus of your looking
I'd be a fool not to know I've lived
forever in these days with your glance
engaged to mine, and my eyes becoming apples
ripening, perfectly attached to the branch of your gaze.

Julie Suk

A native of Mobile, Alabama, Julie Suk also lived in Birmingham, Alabama, for a while. She currently teaches at Queens College in Charlotte, North Carolina, and is associate editor and business manager of *Southern Poetry Review*. Her poetry has appeared in more than forty publications, including *Carolina Quarterly*, *The Georgia Review*, *Greensboro Review*, and *New York Quarterly*. St. Andrews Press published a collection of her poetry, *The Medicine Woman*. She is also the co-editor of *Bear Crossings*, an anthology of North American poets.

Mortal Taste

The year I traced over pictures in *Paradise Lost*
mother complained. What she didn't read
was the body I craved
pitched head-first and naked from heaven,
flesh, and its rabble of feathers,
an unquenchable fire.

Home from the hunt,
father dumped a rucksack of doves
on the kitchen table,
threw one still warm in my lap,
a dollop of blood crusted on its breast.

I fled, but soon crept back
to him sitting there, legs spread,
guts and feathers spiralling down
to mound at his feet,
a tiny wafer of lung lifted on the blade,
doves simmering in a pan
splashed with peppered wine.

Wrapped in fragrance,
I feasted that night, and since.
Now I never see birds
without thinking how shamed
they look stripped but how sinfully good
they go down—like Eve,
her belly, when she left the garden,
lusciously plumped.

Growing Into Hard Times

"Let me see the spots on your lung,"
I ask father.
Home from the sanitarium,
but not allowed to sit close,
he follows me with his eyes.
I am six years old, a show-off,
whirling around his warmth.
He complains I need a winter coat.
Mother nods and smiles,
then talks to the stove,
"And who pays?"
I flatten against the wall,
the year a cat's cradle
of delicate maneuvers,
my father the tangle.

He sings a bitter, off-key song
Just around the corner
there's a rainbow in the sky
and I believe
until the school bus veers into a dog,
and I watch a bloody spasm
smear the road, watch
a war they never thought would come
hit home, the door slam,
my father mutter,
"I should have been called."
Afraid to look his way, afraid not,
I fight and, in my own good time, love,
remembering what he said,
"If you lose the eye of a cornered fox,
it will disappear."

Waiting for the Story-Teller

Once more we wait for the story-teller
to step into the margin and reveal intentions:
why the first letter flowered,
spiralling down the page with intricate designs,
the hand translating what the tongue began.

148

Clues drop, mostly forgotten,
so on and so on stacked like bricks,
crumbling when we look back,
a voice once close now a stranger.

All through the book we wild-guess the villain,
so deceived by this one or that
we look for reprieve, a surprise ending,
the page turning to a house in the woods,
dogs locked up, gun put away.

In the still forest of words,
where the hidden appears in its season,
hills darken and move in.
Like lean horses that have rocked a long way home,
they circle the pool of our hands.
A deer riffles through leaves, then a bird
sings *begin again, begin again.*

Waking the Stars

"I have a new study of a starry night"

The village moon-soaked,
church and spire hunched
like an animal with one ear cocked,
the seething sky crashing blue-black
over stars whitely intense.

I once fell asleep on a beach
and woke in a fall of such stars,
fragments of a dream drifting off,
the moon shrouded as this one is,
only not the improbable orange-yellow-green.
None of this is real,
not the town and its turquoise froth of trees
lapping at the blackened roofs,
nor the ecstatic cypress raking the sky.

The beach, the blanket embedded with grit,
the body lying next to me,
and the name I've forgotten,

they were real, not these fierce stars
staring like beasts at a fire,
nor the sleepers
wrapped in dreams we can't share.

If any one of those villagers
opened a window to look out,
he would drown in that sky:
a flake of plankton
feeding a night that never fills.
It is madness to run through the streets
pounding doors,
waking the dreams locked inside.

Jeanie Thompson

Although born in Anniston, Alabama, Jeanie Thompson grew up in Decatur, Alabama. Holy Cow! Press has published a collection of her poems, *How to Enter the River*, and Baltic Avenue Press has published a chapbook, *Lotus and Psalm*. Her work has appeared in numerous magazines, including *New England Review, Antaeus, North American Review, Southern Humanities Review, Greensboro Review*, and *New Virginia Review*. She is an account executive with the University of Alabama and is married to poet Richard Weaver.

How to Enter the River

Now the singing of the river is his.
He has opened his eyes and each tree
in its green integrity
bows as he moves past.
Beneath him, around him
the water is a muscle,
a heart of jewels spilled over rock.
He's forgotten his hand on the paddle,
his arm, continuous, dips
and pulls, guides the boat
to enter the river, unnoticed.

He keeps his back turned
as his children pry effortlessly
through the rapids,
sure of their skill, that they feel
where the boat must go. Still,
there is a sadness
in his straight, impassive back,
as if by turning from them,
he insures they will go on
paddling forever, forever his,
here among lighted waters,
flexing, opening around him
in song.

for Mickey Landry

At the Wheeler Wildlife Refuge

I. The Observation Building

The little girl in line for the telescope
says, "Look! Them birds are black pepper!"
and turns, grinning, surprised at herself.
Beyond the wall of glass, the flock
rises to light across the bare river bank.

"That bird's crazy," someone whispers.
But the sparrow hawk is dancing in place
50 yards up, wings beating
as if its power draws nothing from the earth.
For a second its wings flash
open, stilled, then it dances again
and falls from sight.

II. Walking the Trail

Winter wheat, rabbit tobacco, sorghum
dried to a dark rattle.
Harvest of sparse color in a dry wind.
And thorns low on the ground,
a network of warning.
Beyond this miniature trail, cornfields
spread green in winter grass.
I stop walking to face the far-off, solid
stand of pines. I tilt my head back:
the air is sweet. Closing my eyes,
I breathe again,
there's no other word,
so I lay my head back, breathing
as deep as a blue-tick hound
when the scent floods past
rank and scared for life.

When I leave this place
I'll take the fourlane
cutting through the backwater.
What tells me I'm alive
is impossible, useless to carry away.

Sue Walker

Although born in Montgomery, Alabama, Sue Walker has lived much of her life in Foley and Mobile, Alabama. She is the author of the poetry collection *Traveling My Shadow* and the editor of *Louisiana Creole Poems*. Her poetry has appeared in many journals, including *New Laurel Review, South Coast Poetry Journal, Piedmont Literary Review*, and *Voices International*. She is a member of the English faculty at The University of South Alabama, and for several years she has served as editor of the literary magazine *Negative Capability*.

Second Hand Dealer

Like the Salvation Army
Death deals in second-hand.
Nothing is ever new.

Death crossed Jr. from Papa's name
that first morning I saw him cry
slumped over the kitchen counter,
his elbow tipping the jug of cream.
All that letterhead paper
engraved *Adam & Son*
suddenly gone as obsolete as flat irons
and starched sheets. My papa—
handed Senior for his name,
handed a blue Packard with running boards,
handed the title, Family Head.

And I remember that hand-me-down day
like I remember A B C,
like the opening of Beethoven's Third,
strong as God strutting the night.
I did not know that Death could hurt
so much or carry on so long, giving
gifts nobody would hanker after.

Papa clasps his walker
aging toward the moment
my turn comes to wear his shoes.

Beneath the Appearance of Green:
Van Gogh, Saint Remy, and Beyond

Doctors pronounce
a clean bill of health—
the way a fold of cloth
hides what was spilt upon it,
visible and real as grease.
Beneath crazed eyes, green
claws the yellow edge of life;
terror paints roads addled as waves.
In Saint Remy where brown potatoes
look with hard blind eyes
at a sky of brooding crows,
Vincent fingers his absent ear
and waits the red explosion of a gun.

Inside McCullers' Sad Cafe

Smoke makes its own statement.
Cousin Lymon brings fire to his lips,
inhales; his mouth makes o-rings
in fetid air. Men gather, women whisper,
children point and sneer. No one eats.
No one drinks. Coffee sediments
pool in a pot on the stove.
Snow fell on groundhog day;
coldness lingers in what observers say:
Amelia's lover took a lover. That's
the cause of this fight. It is why
tables are shoved against the wall.
It is why a man and woman square up
against each other in smouldering
whorls of exhumation.

Eugene Walter

Born in Mobile, Alabama, Eugene Walter is both a poet and a fiction writer. His first novel, *The Untidy Pilgrim*, won the Lippincott Prize and in 1987 was reprinted in the Alabama Classic Series by the University of Alabama Press. His poetry collections include *The Pack Rat*, *Shapes of the River*, *Singerie-Songerie*, and *Monkey Poems*, which was awarded the Sewanee-Rockefeller Fellowship. A new collection, *Smallsong*, is forthcoming. At one time, he served as Assistant Editor to Princess Caetani for her polylingual review, *Botteghe Oscure*, in Rome.

The Socrates Monkey Seen Dancing in Midair, Midst Sun, Moon, Stars, and Field Flowers

In sheer delight of drawing mortal breath
I take such fierce ungovernable pride
That I shall poke my rosy tongue at Death
So he may anger, and you'll hear I died.
Do not believe it, loves, for that round Sun,
If caught and harnessed never could explain
Such coils of Mischief Life as through me run.
(See now the sly Moon greets me once again!)
I prize much magic in my mimic hand
By which I dizzify the day and night:
Now see, stars frolic at my waved command—
Sun, Field Stars, Sky Stars, Moon, all clots of light
For me will sport; O, I am monstrous proud
This life to live, this joy to laugh out loud.

Felix

I

My cat Felix has fur with fawn-colored ground
Whereon some marks are laid in charcoal smudge
But some in fine bold black calligraphy.
His back is sleek, his belly feathery.
His nose is coral, lighter on one side.
Yet those whiskers, eyebrows, struts and filaments,
Are what beseech all wonder and a smile.

155

They're long and they're beautiful, fresh chalk lines
As if some splendid fireworks master
Would indicate to his apprentices what arcs
Gay rockets should describe in some great set-piece
To end a celebration by a lake.
When I stroke him his scimitar claws curl enthusiastic
Like a small roc on an Arabian tree, or Phoenix on a calico.
When Felix yawns all Africa yawns and shows
White teeth in a pink maw. Then hooves are heard far off:
Elands and small deer clattering away.
Don't misunderstand me! I only mean he could
If he wanted to. His white gloves and spats are immaculate,
His jabot always clean. My hands have no scratches.

II

When I was ill, in bed with high fever,
Sweating, tossing, miserable and bored,
He sprang through the bedroom door
Carrying clamped in his teeth a clothes-pin
Which he hid in the bed-clothes.
He pretended not to see me and hid
Five in all then vanished for an hour.
About four in the morning when I switched on the light
He appeared for all the world like a Racinian hero
Saying, hand on forehead, *"Que vois-je ici?"*
Then adding furiously, "Eugene, this house has mice!"
Leaped on the bed, scrabbled in the blankets,
Killed the five clothespins and lined up the wooden corpses
To offer me as trophies of the chase.
The next night he repeated the show,
Did the same number with only four proxy mice.
Later, flat in the hospital, drugged, hearing
Only starchy rustlings of the nuns,
I thought of Felix the mouser-buffo and smiled.

III

He smells good: when I bury my nose
In the back of his neck I sniff
A perfume part broom-grass, part old apple-crate,
A gardener's salt sweetness, a clover spice.
I understand these things in his conversation:

I'm hungry.
Chase me!
Come, lovely loves.
Leave me alone.
Open this door at once.
Why did you move it?
Is that you?
I'm in here!
The moon and I burn.
Keep scratching!
And, of course, the holy hummingbird hacksaw of his purr.
As people grow stupider, more pompous, more tied up
In their own dull viscera, I've come to see with Felix
The importance of a dry leaf scraping across the terrace,
The hallucinating movements of the hawk-moth,
Like him feel irritation at the swallows.
While down below the traffic gripes and scrapes
We watch from this roof the sun descending.
Felix sits straight with paws placed ritually,
His eyes narrow and widen as he glows and says
"King Heat, Gold Friend, I'll wait here for you
Until tomorrow morning." Is there more?
Is not this a very great deal?

Rome, 1970

Scott Ward

Scott Ward, a winner of the Academy of American Poets Prize and a Hackney Award, grew up near Warrior, Alabama. While at the University of South Carolina, he studied under James Dickey, and his work appears in *From the Green Horseshoe: The Poems of James Dickey's Students*. His poetry has also appeared in *Texas Review, Georgia Journal, Southern Poetry Review, Crucible*, and *Due South*.

My Brothers Make a Lantern

All light has left the yard.
Only the sky holds the blue
of light turning back into dark
and shaping in hard shadow every edge
of rooftop, every leaf and treelimb,
shaping my two young brothers
as they sway in silhouette bodies
after fireflies.

A green light opens in air.
They dart with a homemade net
and a mason jar, quick as fish
to trap the insects. Above them
the light of the moon is broken
in tangles of pine, and they appear
and disappear among the trees
far away to the dark of the woods.

Their voices have tapered away
into distance; the forest takes in
the night air. Far off a woman
is calling her children home,
and the sound of a train labors
into the dark. I want to call out
to my brothers, but I see,
very faintly, their light.

This darkness lies thick on my skin.
I move slow under its cover, an outline
in the cool air; I go where the green
spark has shifted beyond the last
boundary of dark, holding my eyes wide open

to take in the field of pure black.
When the green light crosses back to me,
I enclose it inside of my hand.

Slow by a living mantle of light,
my brothers return from the woods.
The circle their lamp is throwing
shows a different side of the night
where objects are one in the darkness
and change in the green of our sight.
I add my fly to the lantern and we walk
in the pulse of that glowing.
I move in the light with my brothers
and feel myself fill my whole shadow.

Hunting in Twilight

I walk among dark shapes
along this bank in the coolly fading
afternoon, the unbroken language
of water staying with me. I kneel
and see the gray light
of the evening, too heavy
to allow my dark reflection,
here where the current runs
against itself, turned
by some obstruction in the shallows, flowing
into a perfect moss-grown laver.

Among the rounded sandstones
a shape fastens itself
in my sight. In the strange refraction
my hand becomes another hand, reaching
into another stream, in a place grown
black and silent with the past.
My hand brings back the stone,
and I am kin to the Creek hunter who waded
the stream all day, searching
for a flint of good dimension,

my hands are one with those that chipped
and knapped the stone

159

into perfection, honed the point
and fastened the shaft with a length
of sinew or thew, I am he who moved
against the wind, stepping ahead
of my scent, drawing
the bowstring to my cheek, my eye
taking sight from the shaft.

The cold of the small stone
seeps into my palm. Some cord
in me snaps tight, unbends the curve
of my imagining. Though I know
I have not passed one night beneath
the stars or walked these hills
in darkness, though I feel no respect
for cold, I would know the burning
of those pure lights, feel my own warm shape
against the world and follow

the shaft's far shadow into forest.

The Gull

She cries, but one could hardly say she sings;
Her wings are fanned transparent in the light,
And she is whiter than the beach she rings

In higher soaring, wind-erratic flight.
Some power of the earth will keep her there.
The sea will take back everything by night,

With windy sounds of animal despair
That contradict the sunlight in her plume,
How every feather holds her on the air.

The shore is like a noisy harrowed tomb.
I walk and wish for other-worldly things,
A voice the rushing sea-sounds can't consume,

For lifting arms, for white embracing wings.
She cries, but one could hardly say she sings.

John Warwick

John Warwick was born in Dothan, Alabama, and grew up in several South Alabama towns. His work has appeared in *Southern Poetry Review, The Chattahoochee Review, The Georgia State University Review, The Sampler*, and elsewhere. He is now studying for a Ph.D. at Georgia State University.

Armor

The landscapes I love are female,
live oaks rising along dark rivers
reaching out heavy arms like old mothers,
their long gray hair between us and the sky.
Missing this, missing any shade
in the white summer blaze of South Mississippi
I drove my tank through the slash pines
of Camp Shelby. No rain for six weeks,
seven hundred horses hammered the woods to powder,
shredding the pines, sweat and gray dust in our eyes
on our tongues, on every inch of our reeking fatigues.
Inside the hot turret, the clamber of metal on metal:
ammo racks clattered, empty shell casings spun on the steel floor
like bottles. When we stopped to fire,
the slam of the breech block,
and the iron muzzle thrusting its long tongue over the pines.
We roared and jolted through ditches, my tank commander,
Bobby Joe McCullough, screaming over my headset
"Slow her down, Warwick, there's a tree. Slow her down!
Damn you, Warwick, you're stupider than hell!"
And I was. Playing soldier,
I drove dust-blind, half-asleep in a dazzle
of sun and crashing trees.
By mid-afternoon, the armor too hot to touch,
we parked beneath a scrub oak
and lay on dust by the treads,
wasps and sweat bees hovering above us,
and dreamed of beer and cool women.
I dreamed of Tuscaloosa,
of low green hills, rivers and rain,
the sky jagged with lightning,
rivers of clear water rising around me
as I lay suspended
as if at the bottom of the sea.

And I swam upward toward the green light
and awoke to the sun blotted out by a wall of rain
and the massed pines roaring like breakers.
Soaked, we crawled inside our armor,
fired the engine and rode home through the blast,
the air electric and cold as glass,
the pines breaking over our armored prow wave after wave.

The Crab

In my mother's house on St. Andrew's bay
I snap open the shells of fried crabs,
brittle pods sweet as pecans from the sea,
the flesh pure white and light as foam.
Outside on the dark bay the moon's long claw
draws the waters seaward toward her jaws.
I mouth sweet flesh and remember
how in this house on the water
my father wrestled, stubborn as Jacob,
for three years with the crab,
until his bones, eaten to cobwebs
by the chemo, fell in upon themselves.

In the dark bay of the blood,
the black crab drifts through the long veins, sleeping,
until sometime it wakens, hungry,
and turns on its own blood,
devouring lungs or brain or bone.

Knowing this, after supper I walk the beach,
the shore pines silent,
the live oaks dark beneath the moon.
On the tidal flats a rotting mullet glistens.
Round blobs of stranded jellyfish stare upward like dead eyes.
I watch the blue crabs scramble from the bay
and clamber in rings around the dead.
High above me the star crab swims through the zodiac.
Around us all the blue rings whirl.

No matter. Beyond us, stars and rogue cells spiral and breed.
And here where the tidal flat ticks and bubbles,
I creep on bare feet softly along the water line.
On the sand around me rings are closing in.

For My Father, Who Never Thundered

From his pulpit my father preaches
under the rush of rain.
In his voice the slow falling of water
washes over the pews.
Through the half-opened windows, Alabama rains.
High above us, it roars on the roof.
A wet gust whips through the water oaks,
streaking the face of Christ as he walks
on sea-green waves of glass
in the window behind the altar,
streaking the wind-ripped sail of the boat,
the face of Peter as he sinks, arms reaching for Jesus,
beneath a storm of glass.
And my father's voice quiet as a river
I wished sometimes would rise in wrath,
his eyes forking blue lightning,
and scorch his astonished Methodists
with a tongue of flame.

The Man-Fisher paced through the rain on the shore of Galilee,
his sandals printing the sand with the shape of a tongue.
All the small boats sheltered in coves,
their dark sails furled and dripping.
And the fishermen huddled under their cloaks,
rain dripping off their hoods,
their dark faces brooding,
as they stared at the wave-swept lake.
And the Man-Fisher walked toward their boats
and called in a whisper of rain,
for he knew when they lay quiet and deep
he could draw up the thrashing soul from the muck.

Now the rain drives down over Alabama
and his pulpit rides above us like a prow.
The congregation sits silent
and deep in their cushions
as my father's voice moves over the pews
with its net.

Richard Weaver

Although born in Baltimore, Maryland, Richard Weaver moved to Huntsville, Alabama, when only two weeks old. After later years in Texas, he returned to Alabama and is now employed at the University of Alabama's College of Continuing Studies. He has served as poetry editor of *The Black Warrior Review*, has twice been a judge for The American Book Awards, and has been a three-time poetry winner in The Birmingham Festival of Arts. His poetry has appeared in *Crazy Horse*, *The North American Review*, *Poetry*, *The Vanderbilt Review*, *Intro 7*, *Intro 8*, and elsewhere.

Awakening in the Language of Pelicans

I've seen them dive and not rise,
or rise and then fall again
lifeless into the sea,
the articulated necks
straight for the first time.
And as they rise

against the wind as they must,
lifting out of their bodies,
the young ones delight into the air,
hissing and squawking as they labor
utterly at ease
with the impossibility of their flight.

I chased one once not yet able to fly,
along the beach and into the surf,
catching him there to draw.
I held him like a child in my arms,
kicking and screaming
until we made the beach. I thought

if I lifted him by his wings
he would calm. But as I did I felt
both wings snap
and he cried out in a pain
I could not draw to lessen my own
until I put a knife in his breast.

Each day I listen to their cries
more and more comes clearly.

They are patient teachers
having waited long upon my silences.
Now if I speak to them
they listen, their heads turned sideways

to the few words I know:
rain-near, fish, sun and moon, man-danger.
If I near their nests
they rise together in a single thought,
a precise harmony scaling overhead,
turning on itself, then settling.

Tirelessly they repeat
what I have failed to understand.
While I sit here and sketch
hundreds drop to their nests.
If they wonder why I return
to walk among them out of the sea,

they are polite enough not to ask.
When they no longer whisper
about the one I killed
I will abide in the wisdom of their mercy.

Flight of the Hummingbird

I watch the waves caressing the beach
and think for a moment
about the time Mary came to me
with the lifeless shell of a hummingbird,
and asked if I could make it fly,
could I make it fly in one place
in one time for once.
How the world remembers
what only comes to light
in the eyes of a child.
I took her in my arms and sighed,
and couldn't help but believe
that everything I feared
would come true.
I wished the wind a true path
beyond the pines. I wished the stars,

the constellations on a turtle's back
would show me a way.
I wished that bird would fly
in a blur of faith, in a whirl of
forgiveness. Forgive me
for what I cannot do, cannot be.

Horn Island

A gull calls out to me but dives
when I answer. I'm close enough now

to hear waves against the beach.
With each oarpull the island

is more a black bar
between the moon and the water's light.

Suddenly, my hair rises and the skiff
yaws. I'm rowing through whiteness

not cold, green water. Bodiless,
suspended in air, in white foam

until the boat settles
as the tideline passes.

How many times have I made
this journey to a barrier island

where earth and sea and sky are one?
To watch the sky overflow into daybreak,

covering me with light; to feel
my soul rock, stone against stone

with the sea, wave after wave,
in the wings of the wind;

to believe as far as I can see
all that I have seen,

that is why I must sing
these praises that the body answers.

A. J. Wright

Born in Gadsden, Alabama, A. J. Wright has had two chapbooks published, *Frozen Fruit* and *Right Now I Feel Like Robert Johnson*, and has had more than 400 poems published in such journals as *Cincinnati Poetry Review*, *Kansas Quarterly*, *Poem*, *Wisconsin Review*, and *New Mexico Humanities Review*. He lives in Birmingham, Alabama, and is clinical librarian in The University of Alabama at Birmingham's Department of Anesthesiology.

the sea and a woman's hands

we sat through the late afternoon
observing changes in the light.
miranda's picture hat,
the tall glasses of iced tea,
a bookmarked volume of proust,
the cordless telephone
and photograph of amy—
these objects defining the patio table
belong in such disguises.

along the artery of sand
a voice from each wave
reaches toward the house
and mimics what's inside us
that resists every language.
miranda talks and talks
about the whitecaps in her life,
when the blood flow peaks
for just an instant,

but the monologue
is a poor imitation
and she knows that.
finally, those hands
fall to the table
like a pair of exhausted birds
that have flown
as far as they can
over a throbbing sea.

a pier of ghosts

out here
on this edge
where the land
walks
over the ocean,
spirits cluster
and name
themselves.
at the end of waves
serious photographs
etch
the sand
like memories
of permanence.

in the rain
figures drop
their fishing lines
of light
over the side
and wait
for the morning's catch.
overhead
a mandala of birds
turns
in the widening day.
on the horizon
communication of skin
has begun.

air born over mars hill

we saw it
early that morning
as we stood
side by side
and almost touching
between the pines
where the fog
had woven a veil
of uncertainty.

we saw it form
and rise
like a sparrow
full of light.
we heard the voice
ascending
from the larynx,
from the earth.
we saw the root,

the final connection
as deep as a spinal cord,
dissolve like a vapor trail.
the words we attempted
fell like chips
from the hands
of a stonemason.
slowly the fog
tightened like a rope.

the final train to america

a vein of boxcars
seven miles long
stretches on the tracks
between two towns,
union springs and eufaula.
instead of hoboes and cargo
this train, as helpless
as a turtle on its back,
supports kudzu and johnson grass
curling over and spiking above the rails
in the august heat
like twin green fevers.

deep in the same afternoon
a few rows of cracked stones,
wiped smooth by the weather,
are the watchtowers of absence.
winter or summer
the stones are cold to touch.

once
children might have clustered
like shadows around the cars
and performed complicated games:
the voices of foot soldiers, Indian fighters
and gunslingers might sail along the rails
like calls of endangered birds.
now
the sun burns a welt of silence
across the skin of every day.

as soon as the stars
prick the evening sky
this train is reaching
its burrow in the dark.
at a table in the caboose
phantom hands
are ghosting a game of poker.

deep in the coming night
former passengers will dream
of the whistles and the rhythms
in the past.

ACKNOWLEDGMENTS

John Allison: "Gardening" first appeared in *Esquire*. Reprinted by permission of the author. Copyright © by John Allison. "Night Animal" first appeared in *Poetry*. Reprinted by permission of the author. Copyright © by John Allison. "Breathing" first appeared in *The Black Warrior Review*. Reprinted by permission of the author. Copyright © by John Allison.

Inez Andersen: "Weep That Wisdom Comes Too Late" from *The Poetry Society of Tennessee, A Book of the Year, 1962*. Reprinted by permission of the author. Copyright © by Inez Andersen. "What Time Is It, God?" from *The Poetry Society of Tennessee, A Book of the Year, 1959*. Reprinted by permission of the author. Copyright © by Inez Andersen. "Go Gentle Into That Good Night" from *Tennessee Voices, 1974*. Reprinted by permission of the author. Copyright © by Inez Andersen.

Gerald Barrax: "Poems Like This" and "All My Live Ones" from *The Deaths of Animals*, Callaloo Poetry Series. Reprinted by permission of the author. Copyright © by Gerald Barrax. "Poems Like This" first appeared in *Callaloo*, and "All My Live Ones" first appeared in *Hambone*. "Eagle. Tiger. Whale." by permission of the author. Copyright © Gerald Barrax.

John Beecher: "Homage To A Subversive — For H. D. T. 1817-1862," "Jefferson Davis Inaugural—Capitol Portico: Montgomery, Alabama," "If I Forget Thee, O Birmingham," and "Undesirables" from *Collected Poems: 1924-1974*, Macmillan Publishing Co, Inc. Reprinted by permission of Barbara Beecher. Copyright © by Barbara Beecher.

John Bensko: "Our Friend, The Photographer at Our Wedding" first appeared in *Poetry Northwest*. Reprinted by permission of the author. Copyright © by John Bensko. "The Craft of the Lame" and "The True Story" first appeared in *The Cincinnati Poetry Review*. Reprinted by permission of the author. Copyright © by John Bensko.

Richard G. Beyer: "The Silent Harbor" first appeared in *The Homely Muse*. Reprinted by permission of the author. Copyright © by Richard G. Beyer. "Reunion" first appeared in *Outerbridge*. Reprinted by permission of the author. Copyright © by Richard G. Beyer.

Margaret Key Biggs: "Below Freezing" and "Three Words in Green" from *The Plumage of the Sun*, Negative Capability Press. Reprinted by permission of the author. Copyright © by Margaret Key Biggs.

173

177